ISIS AND THE THREAT FROM FOREIGN FIGHTERS

JOINT HEARING

BEFORE THE

SUBCOMMITTEE ON TERRORISM, NONPROLIFERATION, AND TRADE

AND THE

SUBCOMMITTEE ON THE MIDDLE EAST AND NORTH AFRICA

OF THE

COMMITTEE ON FOREIGN AFFAIRS HOUSE OF REPRESENTATIVES

ONE HUNDRED THIRTEENTH CONGRESS

SECOND SESSION

DECEMBER 2, 2014

Serial No. 113–232

Printed for the use of the Committee on Foreign Affairs

Available via the World Wide Web: http://www.foreignaffairs.house.gov/ or http://www.gpo.gov/fdsys/

U.S. GOVERNMENT PRINTING OFFICE

91–661PDF   WASHINGTON : 2014

For sale by the Superintendent of Documents, U.S. Government Printing Office
Internet: bookstore.gpo.gov   Phone: toll free (866) 512–1800; DC area (202) 512–1800
Fax: (202) 512–2104   Mail: Stop IDCC, Washington, DC 20402–0001

COMMITTEE ON FOREIGN AFFAIRS

EDWARD R. ROYCE, California, *Chairman*

CONTENTS

Page

WITNESSES

The Honorable Robert Bradtke, Senior Advisor for Partner Engagement on
Syria Foreign Fighters, U.S. Department of State 11
Mr. Tom Warrick, Deputy Assistant Secretary for Counterterrorism Policy,
U.S. Department of Homeland Security 19

LETTERS, STATEMENTS, ETC., SUBMITTED FOR THE HEARING

The Honorable Robert Bradtke: Prepared statement 14
Mr. Tom Warrick: Prepared statement 21

APPENDIX

Hearing notice 62
Hearing minutes 63
The Honorable Gerald E. Connolly, a Representative in Congress from the
Commonwealth of Virginia: Prepared statement 64

ISIS AND THE THREAT FROM FOREIGN FIGHTERS

TUESDAY, DECEMBER 2, 2014

House of Representatives,
Subcommittee on Terrorism, Nonproliferation, and Trade,
and
Subcommittee on the Middle East and North Africa,
Committee on Foreign Affairs,
Washington, DC.

The subcommittees met, pursuant to notice, at 10:08 a.m. in room 2172, Rayburn House Office Building, Hon. Ted Poe (chairman of the Subcommittee on Terrorism, Nonproliferation, and Trade) presiding.

Mr. POE. The subcommittees will come to order. Without objection, all members may have 5 days to submit statements, questions and extraneous materials for the record subject to the length limitation in the rules.

Whether it is ISIS, or al-Nusra, or Khorasan, there are thousands of jihadists in Iraq and Syria threatening global security. In Syria, the influx of foreign fighters far surpasses anything we have even seen in Afghanistan. The scale of this mass migration is unprecedented and it results in deadly attacks.

More foreign fighters have flocked to Syria and Iraq to fight for radical Islamic groups like ISIS in the last 2 years than fought in Iraq and Afghanistan in the last 12 years.

We have a map, I hope we can put that up on the screen, that shows the areas that these fighters have come from. They have come from all over the world. According to estimates, around 15,000 jihadists from over 80 countries have traveled to Syria to fight. Two thousand of these killers are from Western countries, including the United States and the EU; 500 are from the U.K., 700 from France, 400 from Germany, and over 100 from America. All of these Western passport holders can travel freely in Europe and even to the United States once they have finished their tour of duty in Syria.

None of this is hypothetical. We have seen returning jihadists go on murderous rampages before. In May, a returning French jihadists from Syria killed three people during a shooting spree at a Jewish museum in Brussels. In October, a wannabe jihadist who traveled to Syria killed a Canadian soldier. Seven American wannabe jihadists were arrested in the last 15 months trying to travel to Syria to join ISIS.

The senior Obama administration official in September said that some Americans who have fought with ISIS in Syria have returned to the United States. One known example is the case of Eric Harroun. Harroun actually fought with al-Nusra in Syria on an RPG team. On March 27, 2013, he flew to Dulles International Airport where he was taken into custody by the FBI. He was brought up on charges for conspiracy to provide material support to a foreign terrorist organization. He pled guilty of lesser charges and was released in September of that same year. Harroun died of a drug overdose in 2014. He isn't the only American we need to be concerned about.

European jihadists are just as much a threat to U.S. security since they travel freely to the United States under the Visa Waiver Program. I doubt that U.S. and European intelligence services know who every one of these individuals may be.

Just as a side note, the DOD and the FBI were both invited to be here today to testify at this hearing and they would not come.

Some say these individuals will slip through the cracks. Even more concerning is this administration does not seem to have a whole government approach to combat ISIS' global recruitment program. The network is global, sophisticated, and effective. ISIS uses its global network to recruit, fundraise, and smuggle fighters into and out of Syria. This is a much more sophisticated network than anything we know of from core al-Qaeda operatives out of Pakistan and Afghanistan.

The best way to reduce the threat that these foreign fighters pose is to identify how the ISIS recruitment network works and to develop a global strategy to destroy it. We need to understand what countries these fighters are coming from, but also how they are getting into Syria once they leave their home country, the main countries being used by foreign fighters to get into Syria, and what kind of political pressure are we using on these countries to go after these networks? We are not sure what that is. That is part of the purpose of this hearing today.

Complicating issues further, there are a number of Gulf countries who are either unwilling or unable to crack down on jihadists trying to get into Syria. Many of these countries act as the hub for foreign fighters. We need to do more to enlist the cooperation of these Middle Eastern countries to tackle the threat, but we can't do this without a comprehensive plan.

We also need to combat ISIS' online recruitment network. Social media is crucial to the ISIS network of recruiting. They have a whole media center dedicated to producing high-quality propaganda videos, Tweets and the like. This is how their recruitment works: After initial vetting by an ISIS recruiter, travel logistics are finalized. Turkey is the most common-used route and recruiters have extensive contacts on both sides of the Turkey-Syrian border to bring fighters in and out of Syria. So-called religious and physical training begins followed by testing the foreign fighters with small tasks. After that, recruits are given their marching orders to go and fight. They are paid, they have been given weapons. This is a well-oiled machine and very organized. ISIS is only going to get better, more efficient, and more deadly at this and it will turn more attention to attacks on the West in years to come.

I look forward to hearing from our witnesses this morning. I will now turn to the ranking member, Mr. Sherman from California, for his 5-minute opening comments.

Mr. SHERMAN. ISIS is evil and they found ways to convince Americans that they are more evil than other forces in the Middle East. But the fact is that the enemies of ISIS are at least nearly as evil, and I think demonstrably more dangerous to us in the West than is ISIS.

In destroying ISIS, not only is it impossible without huge American casualties—impossible in the present decade—but begs the question, what will flourish in the territory, both the cyber territory, the ideological territory, and the physical territory that ISIS now occupies.

ISIS' enemies include the Shiite axis of Hezbollah, Assad, the Shiite militias of Iraq under Iranian guidance, and, of course, Iran itself. Those enemies also include al-Qaeda, and of course, its fully-authorized branch the al-Nusra Front.

There is talk that ISIS might be able, maybe, to carry on an operation outside the Middle East. Compare that to its enemies. In 1983, we saw Americans die by the hundreds in Beirut. In the 1990s, we saw attacks in South America from Hezbollah and Iran, and there was the attempt by Iran to assassinate the Saudi Ambassador recently right here in Washington, DC.

No one should doubt that the Iranians, the Syrian Government, and Hezbollah have a capacity to get their agents into Western countries and the United States. After all, there is an Iranian Embassy just a couple hundred miles north of where we sit at the United Nations.

As to al-Qaeda, their capacity to carry out attacks in the West was demonstrated on September 11th. And the Khorasan group, which we hit on September 22 was operating in Syria as part of and in alliance with the al-Nusra Front.

So just as important as destroying ISIS is asking: What would occupy its cyber, ideological, and physical space? As to Turkey, we have to urge Turkey to seal its borders and to prevent fighters from joining ISIS, but the Turks seem much more focused on what they see as their enemies, Assad and many of the Kurdish fighters.

They have not allowed us to use Incirlik to attack ISIS unless we alter our policy and decide to use our air force against Assad. Whether we should do that depends in part as to who would take over Syria if Assad was destroyed. Right now, al-Nusra and ISIS seem to be first and second in line, perhaps not in that order.

In addition, the President does not have the legal authority to wage war for more than 60 days under the War Powers Act on the Assad regime. He claims that authority with some support, the authority, that is to say, to go after ISIS on the theory that it is a splinter group of al-Qaeda, and in 2001, this Congress authorized every effort against al-Qaeda.

We must urge countries to seal borders and to deter their citizens from joining ISIS and other extremist forces in Syria and Iraq. We must dispel this notion that the people can go fight, and then return and be monitored. If a foreign fighter returns, they must be imprisoned. And U.N. Security Council Resolution 2178 passed in September requires countries to pass laws, as we have had for decades, that would put such terrorist operatives in jail. That would do a lot, making it clear, especially from European countries, that returning fighters are not going to be monitored, they are going to be imprisoned. It is not only consistent with the United Nations Security Council Resolution, but will act to deter foreign fighters.

Finally, I will be using these hearings to once again urge the State Department to hire people for their expertise in Islamic theology and law, not because a Fatwa issued by the State Department would have credibility, but because the State Department's efforts to persuade legal scholars—Islamic legal scholars around the world—consists of going to them and saying, these guys were terrible, you think of the legal authority, you think of the legal arguments that will allow you to come out against them.

No one would go to an American jurist and say, my adversary is evil; you, sir, come up with the doctrine. Instead, you hire lawyers who know the law and you come to plead not only the justice of the case, but the legality of your argument. And when we get recognized legal scholars in the Islamic world on our side, that will be helpful, but we haven't hired a single lawyer and we are going to courts around the world. I yield back.

Mr. POE. I now recognize the chairman of the Subcommittee on the Middle East and North Africa, Ms. Ileana Ros-Lehtinen from Florida, for her opening statement.

Ms. ROS-LEHTINEN. Thank you so much, Judge Poe. Since the beginning of this Congress, our two subcommittees have held joint hearing to explore the conflict in Syria, the crisis in Iraq, and the rise of ISIL, and we have yet to see a coherent or comprehensive strategy to address these issues from the administration.

For more than 3 years now, the administration has failed to address the Syria crisis head on, and instead has let the country become a safe haven for more and more terrorists who seek to harm the United States and our interests.

We on this committee have continued to sound the alarm and have been pleading with the administration to be more proactive in Syria to avoid a spillover affect that can further destabilize the region. Unfortunately, our calls have gone unanswered. Even former officials from the same administration have been public about their own criticism of the President's Syria strategy or lack thereof.

The longer the administration delays and fumbles about, the greater the danger for both U.S. national security interests and those of our allies. We must have a comprehensive strategy that not only removes Assad from power, but addresses the Iran issue and links Iraq, Syria and ISIL together. All of this does not give me much confidence that our officials have a satisfactory plan in place to address the foreign fighter threat.

While it is important that we refrain from hyperbolic rhetoric and overreaction when talking about ISIL and foreign fighters, it is equally important that we not downplay the threat. The CIA estimated in September that ISIL now has between 20,000 and 31,500 total fighters in Syria and Iraq, and at least 15,000 of whom are foreign fighters from 80 countries.

U.S. intelligence officials have acknowledged the difficulty in providing an exact number saying that, due to "the changing dynamics of the battle field, new recruits, and other factors, it is difficult to assess the precise number of individuals.''

What we do know is that the majority of foreign fighters are from nations in the Middle East. However, there is a significant number, over 2,700 according to DHS testimony, that come from western countries, including over 100 Americans. And as we know, many of these individuals do not need a visa to enter the United States.

The reach of this terrorist organization has extended beyond our initial assessment as we saw in the tragic killing of four people at the Jewish Museum of Belgium, in Brussels, or the attack in Melbourne where, days after ISIL called for attacks against Australians, an 18-year-old stabbed officers at a police station in the hand, body, and head after offering to help the officials with their investigation.

The possibility of homegrown or lone wolf attacks like these inspired by ISIL should be of grave concern to law enforcement officials everywhere. The European Union, which has been soft on terrorism in the past, must take heed of these examples and tighten their terrorism laws, as well as increase their cooperation with us.

We must also remember that the process of foreign fighters joining ISIL and the group's radicalization of Westerners are still in the beginning stages. It took years before we saw the results of individuals joining Osama Bin Laden and al-Qaeda in Afghanistan, and the complete threat posed by ISIL foreign fighters remains to be seen.

Yes, it is true that the problem of foreigners joining a terrorist group is not a new problem, this should not allow us, however, to be complacent. The sheer number of foreign fighters joining ISIL is cause for alarm, and any attempt to downplay the threat is only misguided and dangerous. We must look at all options available to us to prevent fighters traveling to Syria and Iraq from returning to the United States and the recruitment in the first place.

Whether that is tightening travel restrictions on those who try to enter certain countries or come back to the U.S., increasing penalties for providing support to terrorist groups, enhancing cooperation with our allies, especially visa waiver countries that may be vulnerable to tracking these dangerous individuals, all of those are things that we must do.

We have to have a realistic debate about the measures necessary to take on foreign fighters, to monitor them here and overseas, to arrest and detain them before and after an attack, all while ensuring that our civil liberties are protected. Rhetoric that attempts to whitewash the threat or pretend that those who raise concerns are fear mongers does us all a disservice.

I look forward, Mr. Chairman, to hearing from our witnesses about what exactly the administration is doing to tackle this problem in both the short and long term, as well as to encourage a debate we all need to be having. Thank you, sir.

Mr. POE. I now turn to the ranking member of the Subcommittee on the Middle East and North Africa, Mr. Ted Deutch from Florida for his opening statement.

Mr. DEUTCH. Thank you, Mr. Chairman. Thank you, Chair Ros-Lehtinen, for holding today's hearing.

The issue of foreign fighters adjoining ISIS and other extremist groups in Syria and Iraq pose a grave threat to global security and deserves this Congress' full attention.

I want to thank our esteemed witnesses for their many years of service to this country and for appearing here today.

The rise of ISIS has been truly unprecedented. In roughly 2 years, ISIS broke with al-Qaeda, transformed into a well-organized and well-funded terrorist group wreaking havoc across Iraq and Syria. But ISIS has not just focused its efforts on the battlefield; it has developed a propaganda machine that is spreading its message to nearly every corner of the earth. ISIS produces videos, pamphlets, and has generated a disturbing amount of attention via social media.

Whereas terrorist organizations have long recruited members locally, setting up cells in villages, in towns, with Twitter and YouTube ISIS has a direct line across the world. In a grotesque display of disregard for human life, ISIS has used brutal beheadings of Americans as a propaganda tool. Whether enticed by the idea of an Islamic caliphate, claiming to be agitated by the policies of the West, or simply looking for steady income, young men and women from the Middle East, North Africa, Europe and beyond, have signed up to join the fight in Syria. Estimates now put the number of foreign fighters at over 16,000.

Three years ago, we were first alarmed by reports of fighters coming into Syria from other countries in the region, mainly from Saudi Arabia and North Africa. We should be particularly concerned about the alarming number of fighters coming from North Africa.

The chaos that followed the revolution in Tunisia and Libya have yielded two very different results. Tunisia has proceeded with a dramatic transition, struggling at times, but eventually presenting a constitution, elections and a new government.

Libya has been overrun by competing militias, unable to form a strong central government or security force, it is on the verge of becoming a failed state. However, Tunisia's young, mostly educated population has struggled with unemployment, and Tunisia does not have Libya's oil resources to keep the country afloat.

So despite Tunisia's success and post-Arab Spring transition, the country with the largest number of foreign fighters in Syria and Iraq is now Tunisia. The recent Washington Post article examined the factors contributing to the rise of young Tunisian men joining jihadist groups. Following years of religious repression by the Ben Ali government, the revolution allowed Tunisians more religious freedom than ever before. As the article reported, the modern Islamist-led government elected after the revolution granted new religious freedoms after a half century of harshly enforced secularism when the state banned women's veils and almost other displays of piety, and jailed thousands of people suspected of holding Islamic beliefs.

Unfortunately, that freedom was exploited by extremists who want to attack inside Tunisia and begin recruiting in mosques and online. The new government has struggled to maintain a balance between security and religious freedom. I raise the issue of Tunisia to highlight the attraction of jihad for many years, even in what would traditionally be considered moderate countries.

In addition, Africa's proximity and long-standing ties to Europe provide easy transit to the continent and the porous borders in the Sahel countries give radicalized fighters returning home many opportunities to exploit already destabilized populations.

Elsewhere in the Middle East, smaller extremist offshoots are now aligning themselves with ISIS. Terrorists self-claiming allegiance to ISIS have launched multiple attacks on Egyptian security forces in the Sinai. Shiite populations in Saudi Arabia have been attacked by ISIS-aligned groups. There are over 500 foreign fighters from Lebanon, a country already suffering enormous affects from the Syrian conflict.

Our strategy to combat ISIS can't just focus on the battlefield. We must counter ISIS before it grabs hold of youth in Tunisia, and in France, and in Australia, and even here at home. Governments and religious leaders must take initiatives to speak loudly to the Muslim world, about ISIS' perverted brand of religion.

On his return from a visit to Turkey last week, Pope Francis encouraged Muslim leaders to issue global condemnations of terrorism. He told President Erdogan that all Islamic religious, academic, and political leaders should speak out clearly and condemn this terrorism and violence, because doing so would help the Muslim people.

The U.S. and our partners should also encourage training for Imams. The mosque should not be a breeding ground for terrorism.

The State Department is launching efforts specifically aimed at countering the spread of extremism on social media. And Ambassador Bradtke, I hope you will discuss in greater detail the work of the Center for Strategic Counterterrorism Communication.

We must continue to utilize our foreign aid to foster programs that counter violent extremism in schools and among other vulnerable populations. This is a global threat. It warrants a global response. No country is immune to the threat of terrorism. And even as the United States leads over 60 nations in the fight against ISIS, we will always be the face of this coalition, and we must remain vigilant about the threat of radicalization or of lone wolf attacks—similar to the recent attacks in Canada—here within our border.

Again, I want to thank both of our witnesses for appearing here today. I look forward to a productive discussion on this incredibly challenging effort to counter radicalization, stem the flow of foreign fighters in and out of Syria, and prevent future threats to the United States and our allies.

I yield back.

Mr. POE. I thank the gentleman. The Chair will now recognize other members for 1-minute opening statements. The Chair recognizes the gentleman from South Carolina, Mr. Wilson.

Mr. WILSON. Thank you, Mr. Chairman. On Sunday, both the FBI and the Department of Homeland Security issued warnings to American military personnel within the United States regarding possible threats from ISIL. Sadly, this comes after Homeland Security Secretary Jeh Johnson incorrectly, on September 14th, announced: ''At present, we have no credible information that ISIS is planning to attack the homeland of the United States.''

He said this in New York City before the Council on Foreign Relations. This incorrect statement by Secretary Johnson preceded his unconstitutional review of illegal aliens. As a member of this committee, as well as chairman of the Armed Services Subcommittee on Military Personnel, I am grateful to promote the wellbeing of military members and their families both at home and abroad.

National radio talk show host Kim Komando, today in her program during her digital minute worldwide, restated the FBI and DHS warnings of ISIS threats here in America to military families. I look forward to the hearing today on how we can protect American families from the grotesque threat of persons who seek to conduct mass murder of American families in our country. Thank you.

Mr. POE. The Chair recognizes the gentleman from Virginia, Mr. Connolly, for 1 minute.

Mr. CONNOLLY. Thank you, Mr. Chairman. I would hope that we guard against facile answers about Syria. Some of the President's loudest critics, of course, just couldn't quite bring themselves to support his request to retaliate in Syria against the use of chemical weapons. And had the President heeded their advice 1½ years, 2 years ago, ISIL today would be better equipped and better trained, because it drew from the very insurgence the President's critics were urging us to arm and train.

I think there are three questions in today's hearing. What motivates these men and women, especially men, to join this barbaric movement? It is a very troubling question for the west and for Islam itself.

Secondly, how are they recruited? Widely reported accounts of the use of social media, very sophisticated, what is its appeal? Do we understand it?

Finally, what are our options? It seems to me option number 1, priority number 1 is to prevent them from getting to Syria, because once they get to Syria, we have a whole different set of challenges that require a whole different set of answers. So I am looking forward to exploring those questions in today's hearing.

Thank you, Mr. Chairman.

Mr. POE. I thank the gentleman.

The Chair recognizes the gentleman from California, Mr. Cook for 1 minute.

Mr. COOK. Thank you, Mr. Chairman. You know, it is a sad commentary on what is going on in the world right now. Just when you think you put down one terrorist group, there is another one that arises from the ashes. And it is something, I think, that underscores the fact that we must stay ever vigilant. And quite frankly, we have to have a military that doesn't have its budget cut to the bone, and is what is called a C–1 readiness, because you would never know what is going to happen tomorrow.

I have been on this planet a long time, it is probably—Ted, I saw that smirk in your face—it is probably—in my opinion, the world is probably the most dangerous it has ever been since I have been involved in these things. I have been in combat, I have been at war. And now, you strive to go forward and make the world safe, not only for your country, but for your kids and your grandchildren. So thank you for having this hearing.

I think this is something we cannot fall asleep on. And as I said earlier, we have got to be ever vigilant, and we have got to find out what is going on, and I appreciate our folks joining us to give us an update.

Thank you very much, Mr. Chairman.

Mr. POE. The Chair recognizes the gentleman from New York, Mr. Higgins, for an opening statement.

Mr. HIGGINS. Thank you, Mr. Chairman, for holding this hearing. The Islamic State's rapid conquest of a territory covering large portions of Syria and Iraq is, in part, going to the prolific recruitment of foreign fighters who now number an estimated 16,000, nearly half of the Islamic State's fighting force.

Consequently, the integral part of the strategy to degrade and destroy ISIS must be an effective plan to stem the flow of foreign fighters who not only add to the Islamic State's fighting strength, but to also represent a serious terror threat when they return to their countries of origin.

Of greatest concern are the roughly 2,000 foreign fighters originating in western countries, many of which would not need visas to enter the United States or Europe. Until it can be properly addressed, the Islamic State's proficient use of social media and other mediums to continue to facilitate the recruitment of self radicalization of these individuals, countering these threats will require constant vigilance and enhanced coordination with our allies. I look forward to today's discussion with our witnesses and I yield back.

Mr. POE. The Chair recognizes the gentleman from Illinois, Mr. Kinzinger, for 1 minute.

Mr. KINZINGER. Thank you, Mr. Chairman. And to both committees on which I serve, thanks for holding this hearing. And to our witnesses, thank you for being here.

We are bombing ISIS, that is good, I wish we had started that back in January when there were only a few thousand of them. Today we are playing a lot of catch-up. I just recently got back from Iraq, I guess, probably 2 months ago now, 1½ months. When I left in '09, as a pilot in the military, the war was won, and when I went back, just a few months ago, it was very devastating to see.

I hope that we begin to hear from this administration a strategy for Syria. I echo what a lot of people have said. Two hundred thousand dead Syrians today, at least many of which are women and children by the evil dictatorship of Bashar al-Assad, who by the way is no protector of Christianity. He is an evil, bad person, and the incubator of ISIS.

The reason this rebellion exists, the reason people would even be attracted is they see ISIS, in some cases, some people see them as the best alternative to Assad. So I think it is important for us to plus up the FSA and protect them as we allow them to clear their own country out of ISIS. Hopefully we will begin to hear that from this administration. It has been a few years, maybe we will catch some good news here soon. I yield back.

Mr. POE. The Chair recognizes the gentleman from Rhode Island, Mr. Cicilline for his opening statement.

Mr. CICILLINE. Thank you, Chairman Ros-Lehtinen, Chairman Poe, and Ranking Members Deutch and Sherman for holding today's hearing on this very important issue. The continuing threat that ISIL poses to international stability is a serious concern of the United States and our allies.

Addressing that threat with the comprehensive and carefully developed and thoughtful strategy must be a top priority of U.S. foreign policy. It is our responsibility to develop a response to ISIL's insurgency in Iraq and Syria that ensures that all options and their consequences are carefully considered. Even as the administration wraps up its response with a $5.6 billion request from the President to fund the military response in Iraq and Syria, and an operation to train and equip rebels in Syria, ISIL continues to attract foreign fighters, including fighters from western countries.

We must do all we can to stop this flow of foreign fighters into the region. And as part of this effort, we must examine how and why ISIL is successfully engaging foreign fighters and how the United States can best restrict ISIL's access to additional personnel and battle resources.

I look forward to hearing the perspective of the witnesses that we have assembled on these important issues. With that I yield back. And thank you, Mr. Chairman.

Mr. POE. The gentleman yields back his time. Are there any other members on the majority side?

The Chair recognizes the gentlelady from Florida, Ms. Frankel, for 1 minute.

Ms. FRANKEL. Thank you very much for being here. Well, I have to confess just a little bit of uneasiness what we should be doing with ISIL. So there are two issues that have been floating around in my mind that I want to try to articulate.

Just based on some things I have read and heard and I would like to get your reaction as you go forward. One, to pick up own my colleagues who talked about al-Assad and hundreds of thousands of his own people that he slaughtered. And causing many of them thousands to flee into other countries such as Turkey, destabilizes those countries.

I know some who will say that ISIL is the enemy, the fiercest fighter against Assad. So one question I would have is: How do you balance going after ISIL and then are we helping Assad in that regard?

And then the second issue that I have read and heard people say is that our actions, whether it is bombing, air strikes or whatever, that we tend to inflame certain folks that will cause them to use our actions as a recruitment for ISIL. And I would like to hear your reaction to that.

I yield back, Mr. Poe.

Mr. POE. Anyone else wish to make an opening statement? Mr. Kennedy for 1 minute.

Mr. KENNEDY. Thank you, Mr. Chairman. And thank you to the chair and ranking members of this committee for holding this hearing. And to our witnesses thank you for coming to testify today, thank you for your service to our country.

A number of my colleagues have already touched on the issues around trying to limit the number of foreign fighters coming into

Syria and the region, and obviously that is critical. The other aspect to this is our ability to monitor their movements after they are there and once they return home. This puts an awful lot of pressure on our intelligence agencies' apparatus to try to make sure we can successfully identify those who have traveled, and once they try to leave, their routes of entry back into Europe, and potentially back into the United States and Canada.

I would love to hear your own assessment of those capabilities, how much confidence we have in our intelligence communities in order to conduct those operations, if they need additional resources in order to do so, and what road blocks I might see in terms of making sure that they are right every time, and that somebody doesn't slip through the cracks. Thank you.

Mr. POE. I thank the gentleman. The Chair recognizes the gentleman from Illinois, Mr. Schneider, for 1 minute.

Mr. SCHNEIDER. Thank you. I want to thank the witnesses for joining us today and sharing what is being done in a very serious concern. It seems that there are three challenges we face. One is cutting off the source of these fighters. I would be interested in hearing your take, as was mentioned earlier, on why so many are coming from five countries. Five countries represent half the total, Morocco, Tunisia, Turkey, Jordan, and Saudi Arabia.

What is being done to interdict their progress toward Syria and Iraq? How we can prevent them from going and again a discussion how we make sure that they are not allowed to come back?

With that, I yield back my time.

Mr. POE. The gentleman yields back. Anyone else?

I will introduce our witnesses and give them time for their opening statements. The Honorable Robert Bradtke serves as Senior Advisor for Partner Engagement on Syria Foreign Fighters at the Department of State. Ambassador Bradtke has more than 40 years experience in dealing with foreign policy national security issues and previously served as our Ambassador to Croatia.

Mr. Thomas Warrick is a Deputy Assistant Secretary for Counterterrorism Policy at the U.S. Department of Homeland Security. Prior to joining DHS, Mr. Warrick spent several years as an international lawyer in private practice before a decade-long tenure at the Department of State where he focused on the Middle East.

Ambassador Bradtke, we will start with you, you have 5 minutes.

STATEMENT OF THE HONORABLE ROBERT BRADTKE, SENIOR ADVISOR FOR PARTNER ENGAGEMENT ON SYRIA FOREIGN FIGHTERS, U.S. DEPARTMENT OF STATE

Ambassador BRADTKE. Chairman Poe, and Chairman Ros-Lehtinen and distinguished members of the subcommittees. Thank you for the opportunity to appear today on behalf of the State Department at this hearing on ISIS and the threat of foreign fighters. I would ask that the full text of my statement be included in the record and I will proceed with the summary of my statement.

Mr. Chairman, Madam Chairman, the State Department, along with other agencies in the United States Government, is deeply concerned about the threat posed by foreign fighters who have traveled to Syria and Iraq to participate in the conflicts there.

These fighters, many of whom have joined ISIL, al-Nusra Front and other terrorist organizations are a threat to people across Syria and Iraq and endanger the stability of the entire region. They are also a serious threat to the United States and our partners globally. We are concerned that these trained, battle-hardened fighters will try to return to their home countries or other countries and carry out attacks.

To respond to this threat, the United States has been working closely with our foreign partners for more than 2 years. And this summer, with a growing threat posed by ISIL, the United States has intensified its response by building a coalition of more than 60 countries with the goal of degrading and defeating ISIL. General John Allen is leading the comprehensive strategy across five lines of effort, including military support to our partners, disrupting the flow of foreign fighters, stopping ISIL's financing and funding, addressing humanitarian crises in the region, and exposing ISIL's true nature.

Today I would like to describe for you how we are pursuing the foreign fighter line of effort. Not only within the context of our ISIL strategy, but also within the broader framework of the threat posed by other terrorist organizations and groups, such as al-Nusra and the Khorasan group.

Critical to countering this threat is our engagement with our foreign partners. The State Department has been leading a whole-of-government outreach effort with foreign partners, an effort that is being carried out at all levels across the United States Government, including by our intelligence agencies, the National Counterterrorism Center, the Department of Homeland Security, the Department of Justice, the Department of Treasury, the Federal Bureau of Investigation, our military commands, as well as our Embassies overseas.

In my capacity as Senior Advisor for Partner Engagement on Syria Foreign Fighters, I have led interagency delegation visits to 17 countries, from Europe to Southeast Asia, to address this issue with our partners. We and our partners recognize that we must use all the tools at our disposal and cooperate across a wide range of activity.

Let me outline for you very briefly seven areas where we are engaging with our foreign partners. First is information sharing. To prevent and interdict the travel of foreign fighters, we are working bilaterally to bolster information sharing on known suspected terrorists. And we have called upon our partners to make increased use of multilateral arrangements for sharing information, specifically Interpol's foreign fighter fusion cell.

Second is law enforcement cooperation. We are using formal and informal mechanisms to help police and law enforcement authorities in our partner countries bring suspected terrorists to trial.

Third is capacity building. We have worked closely with a number of partner countries, including Tunisia, to help them strengthen their infrastructure to tackle the foreign fighter threat, including stronger counterterrorism legislation and improved interagency coordination.

Fourth is stopping the flow of external finance into terrorist organizations. Together with the Treasury Department, we have aggressively raised with our partners cases where we believe individuals or organizations are raising funds that are used to support ISIL or other terrorist groups.

In recent months, as ISIL is gaining control of more territory, we are also engaging with our partners in the regions to cut off the funding ISIL derives in the sale of oil and isolate it from the international financial system.

Fifth is counter messaging. We have sought to expose the true nature of ISIL and other terrorist groups through the work on social media and the Internet at the Center for Strategic Counterterrorism Communications.

Sixth is counter and violent extremism. In my meetings with foreign partners, I found that all of us are looking for ways to keep individuals from being radicalized. We have been sharing our own experience encountering violent extremism programs which are carried out in the United States. And we are working with partners to build their capacity to engage their own communities.

Seventh and lastly, is border and aviation security. My colleague from the Department of Homeland Security will go into this area in greater detail.

Parallel with this bilateral engagement, we have also joined with our partners in multilateral 4. In September, President Obama presided over a session of the United Nations Security Council that approved the United Nations Security Council Resolution 2178, a binding resolution that calls upon all the countries, among other things, to prevent and suppress recruiting, organizing, transporting or equipping of foreign terrorist fighters, and to take action to prevent radicalization to violence.

Also in September, at a meeting chaired by Secretary Kerry and the Turkish foreign minister, the Global Counterterrorism Forum adopted the first ever set of international good practices for a more effective response to the foreign terrorist fighter phenomenon.

The inaugural plenary of the GCTF foreign terrorist fighters working group chaired by the Netherlands and Morocco will take place in Marrakesh, December 15 and 16.

Mr. Chairman, Madam Chairman, in a speech at West Point, President Obama stated, we must shift our counterterrorism policy to "more effectively partner with countries where terrorist networks seek a foothold."

As I hope I have indicated in this statement, we are engaging with our partners and using all the tools at our disposal in the effort to deal with the threat posed by foreign fighters. A threat unfortunately that will be with us for years to come.

I stand ready to address some of the issues that members raised during their statements and answer your questions. Thank you.

[The prepared statement of Ambassador Bradtke follows:]

AMBASSADOR ROBERT BRADTKE
Senior Advisor for Partner Engagement on Syria Foreign Fighters
Bureau of Counterterrorism, Department of State
Statement for the Record for the Foreign Affairs Subcommittees on
Terrorism, Nonproliferation and Trade, and the Middle East and North
Africa: Foreign Terrorists Fighters
Rayburn Building, December 2, 10:00 a.m.

Chairman Poe, Chairman Ros-Lehtinen, Ranking Member Sherman, Ranking Member Deutch, and distinguished Members of these Subcommittees, thank you for the opportunity to appear today on behalf of the State Department with my colleague from the Department of Homeland Security (DHS) at this hearing on "ISIS and the Threat from Foreign Fighters."

The State Department, along with other agencies of the United States government, is deeply concerned about the threat posed by foreign fighters, who have travelled to Syria and Iraq to participate in the conflicts there. The intelligence community estimates that since January 2012, over 16,000 Foreign Fighters have travelled to Syria from more than ninety countries, including the United States. These fighters, many of whom have joined ISIL, al-Nusrah Front and other terrorist organizations, are a threat to people across Syria and Iraq and endanger the stability of the entire region. They are also a serious threat to the United States and our partners globally. We are concerned that these trained and battle-hardened fighters will try to return to their home countries and carry out deadly attacks. Indeed, we have already seen this happen, as was the case in May with the arrest of a French national, with ties to ISIL, for the murder of four persons killed outside the Jewish Museum in Brussels.

To respond to this threat the United States has been working closely with our partners for the past two years, and this summer, with the growing threat posed by ISIL, the United States intensified its response by building a coalition of more than sixty partners with the goal of degrading and defeating ISIL. In September, President Obama appointed General John Allen to lead a comprehensive and coordinated strategy across five lines of effort including:

- Military support to our partners;
- Disrupting the flow of Foreign Fighters;
- Stopping ISIL's financing and funding;
- Addressing humanitarian crises in the region; and,

- Exposing ISIL's true nature.

Diplomatic Engagement and Inter-agency Coordination

Today, I would like to describe for you how we are pursuing the foreign fighter line of effort not only within the context of our anti-ISIL strategy, but also within the broader framework of the threat posed by other extremist groups such as al-Nusrah, the Khorasan Group, as well as "lone wolf" fighters. Indeed, the horrific recent events in Canada show us that the threat from foreign fighters must also include radicalized individuals who may never have travelled to Syria or Iraq, but are inspired by the terrorists operating there.

Critical to countering the threat posed by foreign fighters is our engagement with our foreign partners. As President Obama said in speaking to the United Nations Security Council in September:

> For if ever there was a challenge in our interconnected world that cannot be met by any one nation alone, it is this: terrorists crossing borders and threatening to unleash unspeakable violence.

The Department of State has been leading a whole-of-government outreach effort with foreign partners to highlight the threat posed by foreign fighters, as well as their violent extremist ideology, and to urge steps to interdict these fighters wherever possible. This effort is being carried out across the United States government at all levels, including by our intelligence agencies, the National Counterterrorism Center (NCTC), the Department of Homeland Security (DHS), the Department of Justice (DOJ), the Department of Treasury (DOT), the Federal Bureau of Investigation (FBI), our military commands, and our Embassies overseas.

In my capacity as Senior Advisor for Partner Engagement on Syria Foreign Fighters, since early March, I have led inter-agency delegation visits to seventeen countries from Europe to Southeast Asia, as well as to our partners in organizations, such as the European Union, the Organization for Security and Cooperation in Europe, and EUROPOL. We and our partners recognize that there is no one solution to the threat posed by foreign fighters. We must use all of the tools at our disposal and cooperate across a range of activities.

Let me outline for you seven areas where we are engaging with our foreign partners.

First is the sharing of information. To prevent and interdict the travel of foreign fighters, it is critical that we and our partners share the names of suspected terrorists and facilitators of their travel. We are working bilaterally to share information with our partners, and to ensure that not only are known and suspected terrorist identities shared, but are actually entered into traveler screening databases and travelers screened against those holdings. We have also called upon our partners to make increased use of multilateral arrangements for sharing information. The United States has also supported the establishment of a Foreign Fighter Fusion Cell at Interpol to help disseminate the names of suspected terrorists, and we have urged greater use of Interpol's database for lost and stolen travel documents.

Second is law enforcement cooperation. We are using Mutual Legal Assistance Treaties and other mechanisms to help police and law enforcement authorities in our partner countries share and develop evidence to bring suspected terrorists to trial. We have also dispatched FBI agents and experienced prosecutors to some of our partner countries, such as those in the Western Balkans, where the experience of the United States in managing complex terrorism cases may help them sharpen their own approach.

Third is capacity building. A number of partners have little or no experience in dealing with the threat of foreign fighters. We have worked closely with these countries to help them strengthen their counterterrorism legislation, for example, to criminalize attending terrorist training camps. We have also shared our own experience with "fusion centers" as a means to strengthen inter-agency cooperation among intelligence agencies, police, and prosecutors. We strongly believe that one of the most important things our partners can do in the global battle against foreign fighters is to strengthen their own security.

Fourth is stopping the flow of external financing to terrorist organizations. Together with the Treasury Department, we have aggressively raised with our partners cases where we believe individuals or organizations are raising funds that are used to support ISIL or other terrorist organizations. In connection with this effort, we have promoted what we call "good giving" to make clear that for those who genuinely want to help with the humanitarian crisis in Syria, there are safe, deserving organizations to which they can donate. In recent months, as ISIL has gained control of more territory, the Treasury Department and the State Department are also engaging with our partners in the region to cut off funding that

ISIL derives from the sale of oil and to isolate it from the international financial system.

Fifth is counter-messaging. As President Obama said to the UN Security Council in September:

> There is no military solution to the problem of misguided individuals seeking to join a terrorist organization. Potential recruits must hear the words of community leaders or former foreign terrorist fighters who have seen the truth – that groups like ISIL betray Islam by killing innocent men, women, and children, the majority of whom are Muslim.

We have sought to get out that message directly through the work of Center for Strategic Counterterrorism Communications (CSCC), which, with its digital engagement teams in Arabic, Urdu, Somali, and English, exposes ISIL on social media and the internet for the terrorist group that is. A number of our partners are exploring with us how they can build their own counter-messaging centers.

Sixth is countering violent extremism (CVE). In my meetings with foreign partners, I have found that all of us are looking for ways to keep individuals from being radicalized and attracted to terrorist organizations. Here too, there is no simple answer, just as there is no single reason why someone might decide to travel to Syria and join ISIL or al-Nusrah. Depending upon their own conditions, traditions, and legal frameworks, different partners are looking at different ways to mitigate the drivers of radicalization, such as reaching out to vulnerable individuals, whether through government, local communities, religious leaders, the media, or by offering help to families, who may see a son, daughter, or brother or sister tempted by the sophisticated online propaganda of ISIL or other groups. We have been sharing our domestic experience with CVE programs being carried out by NCTC, DHS, and the Department of Justice and working with partner nations to build their capacity to engage communities and disrupt the drivers of radicalization to violence.

Seventh, and lastly, is border and aviation security. My colleague from DHS will go into this area in greater detail. However, the State Department has joined DHS in strengthening our Visa Waiver Program, enhancing security measures at Last Point of Departure airports to U.S. destinations, and urging the EU to finalize a Passenger Name Record (PNR) directive as soon as possible and to tighten its Schengen Information System traveler screening process.

In parallel with this bilateral engagement, we have also joined with our partners in addressing the foreign fighter threat in multilateral fora, in particular the UN and the Global Counterterrorism Forum (GCTF).

In September, President Obama presided over a session of the UN Security Council that approved UNSCR 2178, a binding resolution that calls upon all countries to "prevent and suppress the recruiting, organizing, transporting, or equipping" of foreign terrorist fighters as well as the financing of their travel or activities, and take action to prevent radicalization to violence. UN Member States must "prevent the movement of terrorists or terrorist groups" through their territory, and ensure that their domestic laws allow for the prosecution of foreign terrorist fighters. Several countries have already enacted or proposed legislation to permit such prosecution; other countries have stepped up their enforcement of existing laws. We continue to urge partners to meet their obligations under UNSCR 2178, and are offering assistance to partners who may need help in doing so.

Also in September, at a meeting chaired by Secretary Kerry and Turkish Foreign Minister Cavusoglu, the GCTF adopted the first-ever set of international "Good Practices for a More Effective Response to the Foreign Terrorist Fighter Phenomenon." This set of "Good Practices" offers a roadmap for steps to deal with the foreign fighter threat, from radicalization and recruitment, to impeding travel, to re-entry and reintegration. The inaugural plenary of the GCTF "Foreign Terrorist Fighters" Working Group, chaired by the Netherland and Morocco, will take place in Marrakech, December 15-16, to discuss how to implement the "Good Practices" document.

Looking Forward

In May at West Point, President Obama made clear his view of the importance of working with our partners to deal with the terrorist threat of the future. "We must shift our counterterrorism policy," he said, "to more effectively partner with countries where terrorist networks seek a foothold." As I hope I have made clear in this statement, we are engaging with our partners, using all the tools at our disposal in the effort to deal with the threat posed by foreign fighters -- a threat, unfortunately that will be with us for years to come.

I look forward to answering your questions.

Mr. POE. Mr. Warrick, the Chair recognizes you for your 5-minute opening statement.

STATEMENT OF MR. TOM WARRICK, DEPUTY ASSISTANT SECRETARY FOR COUNTERTERRORISM POLICY, U.S. DEPARTMENT OF HOMELAND SECURITY

Mr. WARRICK. Thank you, Mr. Chairman, Madam Chairman, Ranking Member Sherman, Ranking Member Deutch and members of the subcommittees. Thank you for the opportunity to testify today about the efforts by Department of Homeland Security to protect our Nation from terrorists operating out of Syria and Iraq.

I want to address how DHS helps to protect the homeland from foreign fighters who are not from Syria or Iraq, but who travel there to participate in the conflict and who may then seek to attack the United States, U.S. persons, U.S. interests, or U.S. allies.

For today, let me discuss the Islamic State of Iraq in the Levant. I am not going to give this as a full threat briefing on ISIL, that would be best in a classified setting. Suffice it to say that at present, DHS is unaware of any specific, credible threat to the U.S. homeland from ISIL.

However, as has been noted, ISIL has encouraged its supporters to carry out attacks. Such attacks could be conducted without specific direction from ISIL with little or no warning.

In addition, terrorist groups have shown interest in attacks on U.S. bound airplanes. Terrorists have tried to conceal improvised explosive devices in commercial electronics, in areas of the body that they think won't be thoroughly searched, and in shoes, cosmetics, or liquids in order to try to defeat airport security screening.

Let me turn to seven specific security measures put in place in response to the terrorist threat from Syria and Iraq. First, aviation security. In early July, Secretary Johnson directed the Transportation Security Administration to enhance screening at a number of overseas airports with direct flights to the United States.

Subsequently, TSA increased the number of additional airports overseas to use enhanced screening methods. DHS will work with air carriers and foreign airports to adjust screening measures to take account of changes to the threat.

Second, preclearance. One of Secretary Johnson's initiatives is to increase the use of preclearance at overseas airports with flights to the United States. Preclearance means that before a plane takes off, all passengers and their baggage are inspected by U.S. Customs and Border Protection officers, using their full legal authorities, and using enhanced aviation security approved by TSA.

We have had preclearance in airports in Canada and the Caribbean and we recently expanded it to Ireland and the United Arab Emirates. DHS is working with the aviation industry, airport authorities and other governments to expand the number of U.S. bound flights covered by the security benefits that preclearance brings.

Third, tracking foreign fighters. DHS, along with the FBI, the National Counterterrorism Center (NCTC) and the U.S. Intelligence community is making greater efforts to track foreign fighters who fought in Syria who come from the United States or who seek to enter the United States from another country.

Fourth, we are encouraging other governments to collect their own information on foreign fighters. This topic is almost always item number 1 on DHS's agenda with European governments. We are helped by U.N. Security Council Resolution 2178, which has provided a new push for European and other governments' newest technology like advanced passenger information (API) that DHS has long used to detect known and previously unknown terrorists by giving us information on terrorist travel.

Fifth, enhancing the Electronic System for Travel Authorization (ESTA) and the Visa Waiver Program (VWP), DHS is increasing our ability to track those who enter and leave Syria and may later try to travel to the United States without a State Department-issued visa under the Visa Waiver Program.

On November 3, DHS began requiring additional data elements that will allow CBP to conduct better screening and better security vetting of prospective VWP travelers before they board aircraft for the United States. The additional data provides an additional layer of security for the VWP.

Sixth, DHS is continually working to help communities identify Homegrown Violent Extremists. Secretary Johnson regularly speaks of the challenge posed by the independent actor or lone wolf. In many respects, this is the hardest terrorist threat to detect and one of concern to DHS.

We help detect HVEs through outreach and community engagement. Secretary Johnson has personally participated in community meetings in Chicago, Columbus, Minneapolis, and Los Angeles that focus on community concerns and building trust and partnership to counter violent extremism.

Seventh, information sharing within the U.S. Government. DHS and our interagency partners evaluate threat data and ensure relevant information reaches DHS personnel in the field, as well as our state, local and tribal and territorial partners. DHS, jointly with the FBI, releases joint intelligence bulletins to provide context and background for them to use. DHS and our interagency partners work continually to share information with each other about possible foreign fighters.

Mr. Chairman, Madam Chairman, since sanction 9/11, DHS and our partners in the law enforcement and intelligence community have vastly improved the Nation's ability to detect and disrupt terrorist plots. We ask for your support as we continue to adapt to emerging threats and to improve our ability to keep our Nation safe.

Thank you very much. We obviously are happy to answer your questions.

[The prepared statement of Mr. Warrick follows:]

Statement for the Record

Thomas S. Warrick

Deputy Assistant Secretary for Counterterrorism Policy

U.S. Department of Homeland Security

Before the

U.S. House of Representatives

Committee on Foreign Affairs

Subcommittee on Terrorism, Non-Proliferation, and Trade

Regarding

Foreign Fighter Threats to the Homeland in the Context of the Islamic State of
Iraq and the Levant

December 2, 2014

Chairman Poe, Ranking Member Sherman, Chairman Ros-Lehtinen, Ranking Member Deutch, and Members of the Subcommittee:

Thank you for the opportunity to testify today about the U.S. Department of Homeland Security (DHS) efforts to protect our nation from the threats posed by terrorists operating out of Syria and Iraq. Many of these terrorists are affiliated with the Islamic State of Iraq and the Levant (ISIL). In particular, I will address how DHS helps to protect the U.S. Homeland from violent extremists we call "foreign fighters" who are not from Syria or Iraq but who travel there to participate in the conflict and who may then seek to attack the United States, or U.S. persons or interests, or our allies.

While this hearing focuses on the terrorist threat from Syria and Iraq, core al-Qa'ida, al-Qa'ida in the Arabian Peninsula (AQAP), and their affiliates and adherents in other parts of the world are a major concern for DHS. Despite senior leadership deaths, these groups maintain the intent and, in some cases, the capability to conduct attacks against U.S. citizens and our facilities. AQAP and other terrorist groups have shown they can adjust their tactics, techniques and procedures to target the West in a number of ways.

ISIL is one of the terrorist groups operating out of Syria and Iraq. ISIL operates in some ways as a military organization, is attempting to govern territory, and has capabilities most terrorist groups do not possess. The group aspires to overthrow governments in the region and eventually beyond.

At present, DHS is unaware of any specific, credible threat to the U.S. Homeland from ISIL. However, violent extremists who support terrorist groups based in Syria have demonstrated the intent and capability to target American citizens overseas. ISIL constitutes an active and serious threat within the region and could attempt attacks on U.S. targets overseas with little-to-no warning. Attacks by ISIL and its predecessor, al-Qa'ida in Iraq on U.S. personnel from 2004 to 2011 in Iraq are well-known and well- documented. ISIL has also encouraged its supporters to carry out attacks elsewhere. Such attacks could be conducted by ISIL supporters acting without specific direction from ISIL leadership with little-to-no warning. Even before the events of August and September in Syria ISIL's leader publicly threatened "direct confrontation" with the United States in January 2014. DHS is increasingly concerned that ISIL-inspired individuals may choose to carry out attacks in the homeland rather than attempt to travel overseas.

ISIL has an extensive propaganda capability, disseminating media content on multiple online platforms, including social media, to enhance its appeal. ISIL's English-language messaging and its online supporters have employed Twitter campaigns that have been able to reach a wide audience and encourage acts of violence. ISIL messaging in particular is slanted in the hopes of encouraging sympathetic people, including some in the United States, to travel to Syria to fight with them. We are aware of a number of U.S. persons who have attempted travel to Syria this year to engage in fighting there. More than 100 U.S. persons and over 2,700 Westerners have traveled or attempted travel to Syria to participate in the conflict.

We are concerned about the threat of foreign fighters from the United States or elsewhere who might go to Syria, become even more radicalized, and then return to their home countries, including the United States, where they might try to conduct attacks either on their own or in concert with others. Some foreign fighters turn away from violence, but others, some of whom have Western passports, may become further radicalized to violence while receiving additional training and experience, and pose a potential threat upon their return to their home countries or other countries to which they may travel.

DHS is concerned that terrorist groups operating in permissive environments in conflict zones like northern Syria and western Iraq can pose a security threat to the United States and our allies. The terrorists operating in Syria and Iraq have shown a demonstrated intent to attack targets outside of Syria and Iraq and inspire others to carry out attacks in their homelands.

DHS notes, in particular, that aviation is a continuing focus of terrorist attention. Terrorist groups have shown a continued interest in developing ways to defeat aviation security, and in carrying out, or attempting to carry out, attacks on U.S.-bound civil aviation aircraft. Concealed Improvised Explosive Devices (IEDs) remain the threat of primary concern. Terrorists in the past three years have expressed interest in concealing IEDs in modified commercial electronics including laptops, cell phones, printers, and cameras. Terrorists have also expressed interest in concealing IEDs in physical areas of the body they perceive as not thoroughly searched, or areas we cannot search, such as in the body. Terrorists can also use shoes and other articles of clothing with hollow spaces to conceal explosives. Terrorists remain interested in concealing explosives in cosmetics and liquids in order to defeat airport security screening.

DHS Efforts to Counter ISIL and Foreign Fighters

Let me turn to the specific security measures that have been put in place in response to the terrorist threat that has emerged from Syria and Iraq. DHS has enhanced our already robust security measures, taken some actions directly, and instituted others in collaboration with our interagency partners, state and local authorities, the private sector, and our foreign allies.

Aviation Security: First, to address the threats from terrorist groups overseas, DHS has in recent months enhanced aviation security. Much of the terrorist threat continues to center around aviation security. In early July, Secretary Johnson directed the Transportation Security Administration (TSA) to enhance screening at select overseas airports with direct flights to the United States. Since then, TSA has mandated enhanced screening to occur at additional overseas airports. The United Kingdom and other countries have followed with similar enhancements to their aviation security. DHS continually evaluates the implementation of these measures with the air carriers and foreign airports and whether more is necessary, without unnecessarily burdening the traveling public.

Preclearance: Second, over the longer term, one of Secretary Johnson's initiatives is to increase the use of "preclearance" at overseas airports with flights to the United States. Preclearance is an important step to protect the security of U.S.-bound civil aviation. Preclearance means that before the plane takes off, all passengers and their baggage are inspected by U.S. Customs and Border Protection (CBP) officers, using their full legal authorities and using enhanced aviation security approved by TSA. We have long had preclearance in airports in Canada and the Caribbean, and in recent years, we have expanded it to Ireland and the United Arab Emirates. DHS is working with the aviation industry, airport authorities, and other governments to expand the number of U.S.-bound flights covered by the additional security benefits that preclearance is able to bring.

Tracking Foreign Fighters: Third, DHS, along with the Federal Bureau of Investigation (FBI), the National Counterterrorism Center (NCTC), and the U.S. Intelligence Community, is making greater efforts to track foreign fighters who fought in Syria who come from the United States or who seek to enter the United States from another country. More than 16,000 foreign fighters have traveled to Syria over the last three years, including approximately 2,700 Westerners. The FBI has arrested a number of individuals who have tried to travel from the United States to Syria to support terrorist activities there. We are concerned that not only may foreign fighters join ISIL or other violent extremist groups in Syria, they may also be recruited by these violent extremist groups to leave Syria and conduct external attacks.

Encouraging Other Governments to Collect Information on Foreign Fighters: Fourth, we are working with European and other governments to build better information sharing to track foreign fighters who traveled to or from Syria. Whenever DHS officials engage with European counterparts, this topic is almost always item number one on the agenda. The importance of this issue is also reflected by the United Nations Security Council's adoption of Resolution 2178 in September, in a summit chaired by President Obama that addressed the threat of foreign terrorist fighters. This resolution has provided new impetus for European and other governments to use technology like Advanced Passenger Information (API) that DHS has long used to detect known and previously unknown terrorists and terrorist facilitators. We need to ensure that we are doing all we can to identify those who, by their travel patterns, attempt to hide their association with terrorist groups. DHS is encouraging our counterparts in other countries at risk for terrorist attacks to join with us in using information like Advance Passenger Information and Passenger Name Record data to help identify both known and previously unknown terrorists and terrorist facilitators.

Enhancing ESTA and the VWP: Fifth, DHS is already increasing efforts to track those who enter and leave Syria and may later seek to travel to the United States without a State Department-issued visa under the Visa Waiver Program (VWP). Working with the Intelligence

Community, DHS is aware that a number of foreign fighters in Syria have come from various VWP countries.

In response, this fall, DHS strengthened the security of the VWP through enhancements to the Electronic System for Travel Authorization (ESTA). Those changes went into effect on November 3, 2014. ESTA adds a significant layer of security to the VWP by enabling CBP to conduct security vetting of prospective VWP travelers to determine if they pose a law enforcement or security risk before they board aircraft destined for the United States. DHS determined that additional data will improve the Department's ability to screen prospective VWP travelers and more accurately and effectively identify those who pose a security risk to the United States. These improvements provide an additional layer of enduring security for the VWP and facilitate visa-free travel to the United States.

Helping to Identify Homegrown Violent Extremists Through Community Engagement:
Sixth, DHS is continually working to help Federal, state, and local law enforcement to identify Homegrown Violent Extremists (HVEs). Secretary Johnson regularly speaks of the challenge that the independent actor or "lone wolf" poses to security agencies. A Homegrown Violent Extremist is a person who did not train at an overseas terrorist camp, or join the ranks of a terrorist organization overseas, but who is inspired here at home by violent extremist social media, literature, or ideology. In many respects, this is the hardest terrorist threat to detect, and one of concern to DHS.

To address the domestic "lone offender" threat, while also working to counter the life cycle of a violent extremist, Secretary Johnson directed DHS to build on our partnerships with local communities, as well as with state and local law enforcement, in a way that enhances community relationships. First responders, more than the Federal government, have the ability to work with the community to detect potential threats before they manifest themselves violently. Within DHS, we have outreach programs with communities who themselves are engaging youth in violence prevention. Secretary Johnson directed that we step up these programs and he has personally participated in them by meeting with community groups in Chicago, Columbus, Minneapolis, and Los Angeles. These gatherings have focused on community concerns and served to build trust and partnership to counter violent extremism (CVE).

The department has recently increased its CVE efforts under the direction of a department-wide CVE Coordinator. DHS's Office of Civil Rights and Civil Liberties (CRCL) and NCTC developed and implemented the Community Awareness Briefing (CAB), designed to share unclassified information with communities regarding the threat of violent extremism. It is designed to help communities and law enforcement develop the necessary understanding of violent extremism recruitment tactics and explore ways to collectively and holistically address these threats before they become a challenge at the local level. Also in partnership with NCTC, DHS uses a foreign fighter scenario in Community Resiliency Exercises to demonstrate to communities and law enforcement officials how they can help disengage a person from the pathway to violent extremism. Additionally, DHS collaborates with partner countries (such as the United Kingdom, Belgium, Netherlands, Germany, Canada, Spain, and France) to develop best practices in community engagement endeavors that effectively counter violent extremism.

To address the home-grown violent extremist, we must also emphasize the need for help from the public. "If You See Something, Say Something™" is more than a slogan. For example, in September, we sent a private sector advisory identifying for retail businesses a long list of materials that could be used as explosive precursors and the types of suspicious behavior that a retailer should look for from someone who buys a lot of these materials. In light of ISIL's exhortations to attack uniformed service members, and the tragic events in Canada, Secretary Johnson also ordered a reinforced Federal Protective Service presence in several cities.

Information Sharing: Seventh, the DHS Office of Intelligence and Analysis (I&A) is working closely with interagency partners to evaluate threat data and ensure relevant information reaches DHS personnel and state, local, tribal, and territorial partners who can use this information to reduce risks to the U.S. Homeland. To ensure our state, local, tribal, territorial and private sector partners are kept informed of the current ISIL threat, I&A has hosted calls with our partners in recent months to examine the ongoing situation and, jointly with the FBI, released Joint Intelligence Bulletins that provided context and background, and examined the potential retaliatory threat and ISIL's use of social media.

In addition, within the U.S. Government, DHS and our interagency partners in law enforcement and the Intelligence Community are continually enhancing our ability to share information with each other about suspicious individuals.

Conclusion

Since 9/11, DHS and our partners in the law enforcement and Intelligence Communities have vastly improved the Nation's ability to detect and disrupt terrorist plots overseas before they reach the U.S. Homeland. We ask for the support of this Subcommittee as we continue to adapt to emerging threats and improve our ability to keep our Nation safe.

Chairman Poe, Ranking Member Sherman, and Members of the Subcommittee, thank you for this opportunity to testify. I look forward to answering your questions.

Mr. POE. I thank both of you. And I recognize myself for 5 minutes for some questions. The United States is conducting air strikes; how have U.S. air strikes affected the flow of foreign fighters into Syria? If it has. Ambassador?

Ambassador BRADTKE. It is perhaps a question that might be better addressed to some of our colleagues in the intelligence community, but my sense—looking at the numbers—is that it is hard to say at this point what the impact is. It is relatively soon after these strikes are taking place, the numbers that we monitor—the numbers that we track—are estimates at best. And so, again, I think it is probably early to determine precisely what the impact is. It is obviously something again that our intelligence community is looking at and it is possible that in a classified briefing they might be able to give you their assessment. But, again, from my perspective, the numbers can vary for a variety of reasons. Sometimes it is because we get better information from our partners and that results in an increase in the number——

Mr. POE. So we don't know if it is effective or not.

Ambassador BRADTKE. I would say that if the issue is "is this effective in reducing the flow of foreign fighters?" I would say, at this point, I would want to see more evidence before I would come to a conclusion.

Mr. POE. Mr. Warrick, do you have a different answer?

Mr. WARRICK. Well, no. Again, there is an answer to that question, but I think it really does need to be delivered in a classified setting.

Mr. POE. Turkey appears to me to be complicit to some extent of allowing foreign fighters to flow from Turkey into Syria. Would you weigh in on your opinion of what the Government of Turkey, their position is on foreign fighters going through Turkey into Syria? Ambassador, you will be first.

Ambassador BRADTKE. Mr. Chairman, Turkey is a very important partner of ours in the region. We share a very important common interest with them. We have a shared interest in seeing a political settlement in Syria that removes Assad; we have a shared interest in combating the terrorist organizations that are operating Syria and Iraq; we have a shared interest in dealing with the humanitarian crisis, and also a shared interest in promoting stability in Iraq.

Mr. POE. I understand that, Ambassador, but that is not my question. My question is, is the Government of Syria—excuse me, Turkey, complicit in allowing foreign fighters to go through their country and fight for ISIL?

Ambassador BRADTKE. I was trying to explain some of the perspective on this problem, sir. The Turks have more than a million refugees from Syria inside Turkey. Turks have a 900 kilometer border with——

Mr. POE. I have been to one of those Syrian camps.

Ambassador BRADTKE. There are 37 million tourist arrivals in Turkey every year, 37 million. We believe Turkey—we have had an extensive dialogue with them on this issue for some time—is taking steps to try to deal with the flow of foreign fighters.

The Turks have added a considerable number of names to their denied entry list. The Turks are working with us to try to cut off the flow of funding that might come from oil sales to the foreign terrorist organizations.

Mr. POE. Isn't Turkey buying oil from ISIL that eventually comes to Turkey from ISIL?

Ambassador BRADTKE. There is considerable traffic that we have discussed with Turks across the border. Again the latest information is the Turks are taking steps to try to deal with——

Mr. POE. Are they buying oil from ISIS?

Ambassador BRADTKE. If you are saying, is the Turkish Government buying oil from ISIS? No. If you are saying, is there smuggling taking place across the border? The answer is yes. That is the issue we are trying to deal with is to cut off working with the Turks. The other thing I would mention is the sharing of information with Turkey. I think we are seeing much better information sharing with Turkey with the United States, also with our European partners.

Mr. POE. So they are not complicit, that is really my question. Are they not complicit?

Ambassador BRADTKE. My answer is no, they are not complicit.

Mr. POE. Social media. We know it is obvious recruitment is being done in a very effective manner, it appears through social media. There is the argument by some in our law enforcement agencies not to shut down social media because that is how they track and keep up with terrorist organizations and individuals.

What is your opinion on that? Doing more, or less, or leaving it alone? The issue of all of social media, how it is effective in tracking and the recruiting of terrorists to join ISIL. Should we be proactive to try to shut that network down? Legally, of course. Or should we just do what a law enforcement says: We want to watch this to see where these guys are going. What is your opinion on that, Ambassador? And then get Mr. Warrick and then that will be it.

Ambassador BRADTKE. The issue of freedom of the Internet, freedom of expression on the Internet is one that goes well beyond my responsibilities. We clearly watch very closely the use of the Internet by these organizations, we have a dialogue with the service providers in cases where the posts that are being used, the use of social media counts is, perhaps in our view, contrary to the terms of service. So again, this is a complex question, this is a complicated question, it goes well beyond my responsibilities.

Certainly any use of the Internet for illegal activities, such as fundraising or excitement to violence, is something we take strong legal action against. There are gray areas here of the use of Internet and social media and the question is how one responds to that.

I think we also believe that if you shut down one site, you shut down one account, the chances of that popping back up somewhere else are quite high and quite great. So the other tool we use is counter messaging ourselves through the Center for Strategic Counterterrorism Communications that was mentioned earlier. We try to put out counter messaging on social media, on the Internet to push back in that way rather than simply try to take down the message that they are putting out.

Mr. POE. Mr. Warrick, I will let you put that in writing since we are out of time.

I am going to have to recognize the ranking member, Mr. Sherman, for his 5 minutes.

Mr. SHERMAN. Thank you. Let me first clarify a statement I made toward the end of my opening statement. The State Department has thousands of experts in American law, you don't particularly need more. We also have experts in international law. Those experts help us persuade Western countries of the righteousness of our positions.

I have been pushing on the State Department for, I think the better part of a year, to hire an expert in Islamic law. And the response I get is: Well, we hope Islamic jurists will issue statements that are helpful to us and we will just call them and ask them to come up with something on their own. Or, now and then we will call a professor of Islamic law and get all the information, we don't need to hire anybody.

And so I analogized that to what you would do if you were trying to persuade an American jurist. Would you contact an American jurist and just say, "My cause is just, please come up with the legal theories and support me"? Would you just rely on hiring or whatever free advice you could get from a professor on the phone? Or would you hire somebody who is an expert in American law to try to get an American jurist to issue a statement helpful to you?

It is incredibly important that we get Islamic scholars, experts, and jurists to issue rulings adverse to ISIS and favorable to the United States. It is about time that the State Department hire its first Islamic legal expert to work full-time on that, maybe a couple. And it is time that at least somebody be hired at the State Department, not because they went a fancy American school or because they did well on the foreign service exam.

Ambassador, Security Council Resolution 2178 requires U.N. members to criminalize those who go to Syria and Iraq to fight with the extremists. Have our European allies, particularly visa waiver countries, complied with that?

Ambassador BRADTKE. If I may just comment briefly on your first point about Islamic lawyers, Islamic scholars.

Mr. CONNOLLY. Ambassador, please move the mic closer.

Mr. SHERMAN. I have limited time, so I will ask you to address my question first.

Ambassador BRADTKE. Your question about——

Mr. SHERMAN. Yes, Resolution 2178, U.N. Security Council.

Ambassador BRADTKE. We have demarched all of our partners, through our Embassies in Europe and elsewhere, to engage with these countries on implementing 2178.

Mr. SHERMAN. Can you provide, for the record, a list of which visa waiver countries are in compliance, which have promised to become in compliance, and which are not in compliance that have made no very serious promise to us?

Ambassador BRADTKE. We have had 2 months, sir, since the resolution was passed. The legislative process is in many countries——

Mr. SHERMAN. I didn't—I am just asking for a chart.

Ambassador BRADTKE. I will be happy to provide a list of countries.

WRITTEN RESPONSE RECEIVED FROM THE HONORABLE ROBERT BRADTKE TO
QUESTION ASKED DURING THE HEARING BY THE HONORABLE BRAD SHERMAN

Key Partner Countries' Updates to Counterterrorism Legislation

Country	Status of Legislation Related to Countering Foreign Fighters Participating in the Syria and Iraq Conflicts
Australia	In October 2014, Australia passed a new law aimed at preventing young people from travelling overseas and becoming radicalized. On December 5, Foreign Minister Bishop used this law to ban travel by Australian citizens to Al-Raqqa province Syria without a legitimate purpose. This is the second of three sets of new counterterrorism laws.
Austria	The Austrian government is considering several legislative reforms to address the foreign fighter challenge, including but not limited to prohibiting foreign funding for mosques and requiring proof of parental permission for minors traveling to the Near East.
Czech Republic	The Government of the Czech Republic believes that it is at a low risk of a foreign fighter threat and is not focused on legislative reforms to address the issue, believing it has the tools in place to address any concerns.
Belgium	The Belgian government has been considering legislative reforms since October to address the foreign fighter challenge, including but not limited to stripping alleged fighters with dual nationality of their Belgian citizenship and residency.
Brunei	The Government of Brunei has expressed interest in establishing legislation to counter foreign fighters, but specific proposals have yet to materialize.
Denmark	The Government of Denmark announced a strategy in September to counter foreign fighters, including banning fighter-related travel, sentences including imprisonment, and a hotline for those concerned about foreign fighter activity.
Estonia	The Estonian government is considering potential legislative reforms to prevent nationals from participating in foreign fighter-related conflicts.
Finland	Finland's government implemented reforms in October to criminalize receiving terror training, and is now considering whether more changes are needed in light of UNSCR 2178.
France	The Government of France passed legislation in November to ban their citizens' travel when suspected of being motivated by terrorist intent, as well as prohibiting online recruitment. The first arrests under this legislation occurred on November 26.

Germany	Germany's government is considering legislative reforms to further criminalize foreign fighter-related activities and impede travel. In addition, Germany's Ministry of Interior issued a ban on September 12, 2014, on activities related to the "Islamic State," as well as the names ISIS and ISIL. Germany also recently updated its penal code to make terrorist financing a separate offense in order to facilitate additional prosecutions.
Greece	Greece is establishing a committee which will be charged with reviewing terrorism legislation.
Hungary	The Government of Hungary believes that it is at a low risk of foreign fighter threat, is not focused on legislative reforms to address the issue, and believes it has the tools in place to address any concerns.
Italy	The Government of Italy is considering legislation that would criminalize transport of persons and material to support armed conflict, and that would enhance investigation capabilities.
Iceland	The Government of Iceland is studying ways to implement UNSCR 2178.
Ireland	The Government of Ireland has drafted an amendment to its Criminal Justice Law, with foreign fighter language under consideration.
Japan	Japan's Diet enacted legislation in November to freeze assets of individuals and groups involved in terrorist activities, as well as to criminalize terrorist financing.
Latvia	The Government of Latvia is considering foreign fighter-related legislation.
Luxembourg	The Government of Luxembourg is considering potential legislative reforms that may address the foreign fighter challenge.
Malta	Malta is reviewing ways in which to implement UNSCR 2178 and criminalize foreign fighter activity.
Netherlands	Legislation under consideration by the Dutch government would strip Dutch citizenship from dual nationals engaged in terrorist activity. In addition, the Netherlands has criminalized traveling for the purpose of joining a terrorist organization.
New Zealand	Legislation passed by the Government of New Zealand in December 2014 addresses the foreign fighter challenge, largely through measures to prevent its nationals from departing New Zealand to engage in conflicts and enhancing domestic security.
Norway	The Government of Norway is currently developing legislation to criminalize foreign fighting. This is part of the Norwegian Government's Action Plan against Radicalization and Violent Extremism, announced in May 2014.

Portugal	Portugal does not have specific FTF legislation. However, they have a law on counterterrorism that makes it a criminal offense to join, abet, encourage, recruit for, or train with a terrorist organization, and this law applies extra-territorially. The Portuguese government has begun to explore the possibility of implementing additional measures.
Singapore	No legislation is under consideration at present.
Slovakia	Slovakia is reviewing legislation.
Slovenia	Legislation under consideration since December 2014 in Slovenia would criminalize support for terrorist organizations outside Slovenia, including recruitment, training, and fighting for terrorist organizations.
Spain	The Government of Spain has been considering an amendment to its penal code since October 2014 to criminalize fighting in conflicts abroad on behalf of designated organizations.
Switzerland	In October 2014, Switzerland outlawed all support for ISIL, including propaganda, fundraising, and recruiting.
United Kingdom	The government presented legislation to Parliament in November 2014 that would prohibit foreign fighters from entering the United Kingdom, prevent their nationals from departing to engage in conflicts, and strengthen counter-radicalization programs.
Canada*	In October 2014, the Government of Canada passed legislation to expand warrant-seeking capacity and reform its investigations capabilities.
*Note: Canada is not a member of the Visa Waiver Program but is subject to a waiver of visas for its nationals based on a bilateral agreement.	

Mr. SHERMAN. Their legislative process may be slow, but I know your staff will be fast and get a chart for our record and then we will identify what those countries. Likewise, if you could provide a second chart of Islamic, particularly Arab states, particularly the five the gentlemen from Illinois identified as the major senders of foreign fighters, whether they have passed laws that would criminalize going to Syria or Iraq and fighting with al-Nusra or ISIS.

Ambassador BRADTKE. I would be happy to do that.

WRITTEN RESPONSE RECEIVED FROM THE HONORABLE ROBERT BRADTKE TO
QUESTION ASKED DURING THE HEARING BY THE HONORABLE BRAD SHERMAN

Morocco	• Morocco has had strong counterterrorism legislation since 2003, including preparation for or commission of a terrorist act, as well as a range of weapons offenses. Morocco's 2011 law to expand the definition of terrorist financing has broadened the investigative scope to increase investigation and prosecution of terrorist facilitation. There is a draft counterterrorism law under parliamentary review, but it has not yet passed; the bill would incriminate joining or attempting to join armed groups and training camps in "hotbeds of tension." • Proposed penalties include 5-15 years in prison and steep fines.
Tunisia	• A 2003 anti-terrorism law has extraterritorial provisions that criminalize terrorist activities, including receiving training for terrorist activities outside of Tunisia. The government has prevented potential foreign fighters from leaving the country, on the grounds that that it could threaten national security. The newly seated Tunisian parliament intends to consider an updated anti- terrorism law in 2015. • The 2003 stipulates that anyone who joins a terrorist group or who calls for the perpetration of a terrorist act is subject to 5-12 years in prison.
Jordan	• Jordanian law specifically outlaws supporting, fighting with, attempting to join, or recruiting for any armed group or terrorist group. • Penalties range from a minimum five years hard labor for supporting terrorism, to life sentences for attacks that damage public or private property, or disrupt communications. The death penalty can be applied in cases resulting in fatalities, or if weapons of mass destruction (to include poisons and explosives) are used in any attack.
Saudi Arabia	• The Kingdom of Saudi Arabia has specifically criminalized fighting overseas, attempting to travel for such a purpose, or enabling, recruiting, or

	• encouraging others to do so since February 2014, providing for sentences of up to 20 years imprisonment for violations. • Even before this, the Saudi government discouraged and prosecuted their citizens for "joining illegal groups" fighting in Syria.
Turkey	• In cooperation with foreign fighter-source countries, Turkey continues to develop its "no-entry list," which they report has reached over 7,300 individuals as of last month. • The Turks also report they have refused entry to or deported more than 1,000 individuals suspected of intending to engage in foreign fighter activity. • Turkey has a counterterrorism law enacted in 1991 and subsequently amended. It is not specifically directed against the foreign fighter problem.

———

Mr. SHERMAN. But I take it from your answer that we are doing everything we can to push our friends in the Arab world and Europe——

Ambassador BRADTKE. There are countries that have already in place, as we do, laws that prohibit, that criminalize, for example.

Mr. SHERMAN. Are there any countries that have said, no, we will just let these folks come back and we will monitor them?

Ambassador BRADTKE. No country has taken such a cavalier attitude toward fighters. There are countries that do believe that some of the fighters who come back have been disillusioned by their experience, participated in no terrorist activities while they were in Syria. And they believe in this case, those fighters should been monitored rather than incarcerated. That is a decision that those countries make based upon the evidence available.

Mr. SHERMAN. Is that in compliance with U.N. Resolution 2178, that view?

Ambassador BRADTKE. I am not a lawyer myself. I would have to take a look at that issue, but I think that there are different approaches to how you deal with returning fighters, particularly ones who have not carried out——

Mr. SHERMAN. Look, I don't care if you are just peeling potatoes in the mess, if you are part of the ISIS Army, you belong in prison until this war against Islamic extremism is over. That seems to be what U.N. Security Council Resolution 2178 said, and I hope you will add to your chart a list of those countries that have told us that we do not think that we should criminalize those of our citizens and residents who went to ISIS, joined the army, but say they didn't actually kill anybody.

Ambassador BRADTKE. There is also an issue, sir, being able to prove in a court of law this kind of activity.

Mr. SHERMAN. That is fine.

Ambassador BRADTKE. Have people on the ground in Syria who can come to a courtroom to testify.

So, again, I think our partners use different tools, depending upon what they know about a particular individual in the case. That is all I would say.

Mr. SHERMAN. I yield back.

Mr. POE. The Chair recognizes the gentlelady from Florida for 5 minutes.

Ms. ROS-LEHTINEN. Thank you so much, Mr. Chairman.

ISIL's reach into the United States has been documented. We also know that ISIL is known to be tech savvy, as we have discussed, has used social media tools to its advantage to help recruit foreign fighters to its cause.

And we have seen ISIL graffiti here in DC, pictures of individuals holding the group's symbol in front of U.S. landmarks, including the White House.

And, Mr. Warrick, you testified that DHS is "unaware of any specific credible threat to the U.S. Homeland from ISIL."

Following up on what Mr. Wilson said in his opening statement, on Sunday, DHS and FBI issued a joint bulletin urging our servicemembers to scrub their social media accounts, to use caution with their posts.

Is there a specific threat to our servicemen and -women, most of whom are stationed here in America?

And I will have you hold that thought.

On funding, ISIL is known to finance its operations from a variety of sources, including illicit oil sales, extortion, organized crime, selling of ancient artifacts, donations from of outside sources. We have seen terrorist groups like Hezbollah fund their terror activities through the sale of drugs, often from sources in the western hemisphere.

What are we doing to target ISIL's funding? What kind of ISIL collaboration with drug cartels? Is there any evidence of that, especially here in our hemisphere? And, if so, what are we doing to fight this?

And, lastly, on our allies. In order to defeat ISIL, we are going to need full cooperation with our coalition partners, especially those from the Middle East. The ministers of the GCC, the Gulf Cooperation Council, have scheduled multiple meetings to discuss the ongoing threat of ISIL and possible ways to fight this terrorist entity.

And just yesterday Bahrain foreign ministers announced that the Gulf States are setting up a joint military command based in Saudi Arabia to not only counter the ISIL threat, but the threat from Iran as well.

So I will ask: In what ways are we working with the Gulf nations to fight this radical Islam ideology? And is this joint command a signal that they may be willing to put boots on the ground in Syria?

Mr. WARRICK. Thank you very much, Madam Chairman.

Let me start on that, and then, obviously, Ambassador Bradtke will have things to say about the last part.

First, I am going to do this in reverse order—on the ISIL funding issue, that question actually probably would be best addressed to the Treasury Department. Under Secretary Cohen and Assistant

Secretary Glaser are working very intensively in efforts to try to address the ISIL funding issue. DHS plays a small role in that in terms of criminal investigations about funding activities that go on.

Ms. ROS-LEHTINEN. Is there a specific threat to our servicemen and -women?

Mr. WARRICK. I am working backwards to that one.

On that one, let me go back to what we said over the weekend. There were statements—public statements—by ISIL in September to the effect of calls for attacks against U.S. servicemembers, U.S. officials, and members of the intelligence community.

We are not aware of any specific threat saying that, at a particular time, there would be an attack on a particular servicemember. But we really do want to be able to have members of the State and local law enforcement and members of the military community and their families take certain reasonable precautions to further reduce the risk of any types of events taking place.

We are very mindful of the techniques of the use of social media that you described and that ISIL is able to use. And, obviously, they are able to survey social media as well as themselves.

Ms. ROS-LEHTINEN. Thank you.

Ambassador, on the issue of our allies, are they fighting back this radical Islam ideology? And do you have any info about whether they are willing to put boots on the ground in Syria?

Ambassador BRADTKE. Well, we have a very close partnership with the countries in the Gulf. They are members of this coalition that I mentioned of 60 countries that General Allen has worked to put together.

A number of them are carrying out air strikes in Iraq. So we are getting that kind of assistance from them. We are working very closely with them to cut off funding.

I was in Kuwait and Qatar over the summer. Qatar has just passed a new law on private charities which will try to be more effective in regulating the flow of funding in cases where individuals have contributed money, thinking it was going to some humanitarian cause and was ending up going to a terrorist organization. So they are taking steps in that regard.

They are also working with us on the counter-messaging front. There was just a conference in Kuwait that Under Secretary of State Stengel went to where we talked about what we are doing on counter-messaging, how we are working through the Center for Strategic Counterterrorism Communications.

A number of our partners in the Gulf are interested in setting up similar operations, perhaps, or having a regionally based counter-messaging operation. So, again, we have a very close partnership with them.

Ms. ROS-LEHTINEN. Thank you. My time is up.

But is the graffiti that we have seen in DC and other cities—are those legitimate or do you think that they are not?

Mr. WARRICK. That would actually be a question that I think would be better addressed by either the FBI or domestic law enforcement. They would be able to help you with that.

Mr. POE. Chair recognizes the gentleman from Florida, Mr. Deutch, for 5 minutes.

Mr. DEUTCH. Thank you, Mr. Chairman.

Ambassador Bradtke, I would just like you to pick up where you left off on your discussion of counter-messaging, on the conference that just took place, on the Center that we have in place.

Can you speak in a little more detail about the efforts that we are undertaking, our friends from around the world who are sharing those efforts with us, and how do we determine whether we are being successful? And is there any evidence at this point that we are?

Ambassador BRADTKE. Let me say, as someone who has worked for a long time in the State Department and the United States Government, I find the Center for Strategic Counterterrorism Communications a very interesting and really unique operation.

It is an effort to push back in a very direct, very blunt, forthright way, putting out some very tough messages on the Internet, on social media.

The kinds of themes that are used include putting on social media the atrocities that al-Qaeda and ISIL are carrying out so people can see the true nature of ISIL.

They highlight the fact that the main victims of ISIL are Muslims so that the people understand that this is not a way of helping other Muslims, that, in fact, these organizations are killing other Muslims.

They talk about what ISIL and other groups are doing to local populations, Sunni tribes, others. So, again, very powerful, very direct messages.

Some of the numbers in the last period of time, perhaps the last 10 or 12 months—they have done 25 videos. They have put out more than 1,000 anti-ISIL posts or tweets.

And the way that we have some sense this is having an impact—there are actually two ways. One, you get a number of hits on the sites, the number of followers to the CSCC's operations. The other way is the efforts by ISIL and these groups to take down the CSCC's sites through hacking.

So they are obviously worried that our message is getting out. They are obviously worried enough that they actually want to take action to do something about it.

Other countries have been very interested in what we are doing. We have had a number of countries, ranging from Belgium and France to some of our North African partners, who have come to visit the CSCC's operation here in Washington.

As I said, we had this conference in Kuwait where our partners in the Gulf and other places are looking at whether they can do something similar.

The European Union is interested in trying to get its own counter-messaging up and running. The EU is providing funding for the U.K., which has a counter-messaging program, to try to explain and share its experience with other EU member States.

So, again, this whole area of counter-messaging is very active. My own sense is we can't know for sure whether some individual has seen something on our Web site and has said, "That is the true nature of ISIL and I won't go to Syria," but the fact that we get hits on the site, the fact that the site has been subject of hacking by these groups, indicates to me that there is some effectiveness here.

Mr. DEUTCH. Can you share with us how many times the videos have been viewed, how many hits there have been either on the— the posts, how many tweets have been viewed?

Ambassador BRADTKE. I would be happy to get that for the record so I have the latest information.

The Center for Strategic Counterterrorism Communications' (CSCC) Arabic language videos were viewed 959,187 times from June 10 to December 5, 2014. Urdu videos were viewed 3,947 times and Somali videos 26,676 times.* Combined numbers of tweets for the Arabic, Urdu, and Somali languages from January 1 to December 1, 2014 were 25,844 with a total reach of over 7.3 million.

CSCC launched its pilot English Language Initiative (ELI) on Twitter in August, 2013 and began messaging on Facebook in August, 2014. Twitter followers reached 19,100 from August 2013 to November 2014. The number of followers for CSCC's English Facebook page rose to 8,868 from August 2014 to November 2014. The English YouTube account, which launched in August 2014 rose to 2,840 followers in November, 2014. There have been 3,150 tweets with total impressions of 12.2 million, 315 Facebook posts with a total reach of 678,000, and 14 YouTube videos with total views at 1,003,000.

*These numbers do not include numbers for Vimeo accounts (access to those figures is a fee-based service).

Mr. DEUTCH. Okay. And you said that the U.K. has a center. Is the work that we are doing meant strictly—who are we focusing on? And, clearly, I would imagine the message would be slightly different targeting an Australian audience than a Belgian audience or America.

Ambassador BRADTKE. And that is why we think it is important that other countries develop a capability. The CSCC is doing its efforts in three languages: Arabic, of course; Urdu, because of its messaging that goes beyond the Syrian-Iraq front; and then English as well.

The English messaging is a more recent development. But, as you say, there are needs for others—for example French. We know the fighters in Belgium, France. And that is why we think it is important that other countries also develop this capability.

Mr. DEUTCH. And in my remaining seconds, Mr. Warrick, this may be something that you will be able to respond to in your discussions with some of my colleagues. If not, if you could respond in writing after.

Your testimony about the efforts by the Secretary to increase the use of preclearance at overseas airports, I would very much like to know what the plan is, what airports we have targeted, by when, and how many we have already put in place to date.

Mr. WARRICK. Thank you very much.

Actually, that is a question we would prefer not to address in an open session. You will appreciate the sensitivity, not just in terms of discussions with foreign partners, but we have no intention of laying out a roadmap of where we are not because of what effect that might have on the thinking of our adversaries. But in a closed setting, we can get someone who can give you a great deal more information on that.

Mr. DEUTCH. I was only following up on the countries identified in your testimony. But I look forward to discussing that in the appropriate setting.

Mr. WARRICK. Where we have it, it is obviously a public matter and people see our officers in their uniforms.

Mr. DEUTCH. Thank you.

I yield back.

Mr. POE. Chair recognize the gentleman from South Carolina, Mr. Wilson.

Mr. WILSON. Thank you, Judge Poe.

And thank you, Chairwoman Ros-Lehtinen, for this joint subcommittee hearing today. This is very important.

Both of your testimonies have been very enlightening. But I am just very concerned. The American people need to know, as the President, I believe, is ignoring the jihadist threat, that ABC News, of all people, Monday night reported, "The day before the U.S. launched its biggest air blitz against the terrorist group in Iraq and Syria in late September, ISIS spokesman Abu Mohammad al-Adnani called upon Muslims in the U.S. And Europe to attack members of the military."

The direct quote: "Do not ask for anyone's advice and do not seek anyone's verdict. Kill the believer, whether he is a civilian or military, for they have the same ruling. Both of them are disbelievers. Both of them are considered to be waging war," Adnani said in an audio speech posted online on September the 21st.

Mr. Warrick, what is your current threat assessment of an attack by a domestic jihadist or foreign fighters on the U.S. homeland?

Mr. WARRICK. Thank you very much.

That statement was posted in social media by a foreign participant attributing it to Adnani, as you said.

Obviously, he was not in the homeland when the statement was made, but he was intending that his message reach out to prospective sympathizers here in the United States.

There are obviously a number of things that DHS tries to do to prevent people from becoming radicalized to violence. This is through the community efforts which I addressed in my testimony.

In addition, there are other steps that other law enforcement organizations, like the FBI, do in terms of trying to track activity and where there are steps, especially toward foreign travel, that prospective sympathizers may make. Then this gets them on the radar screen of people at DHS.

So there are a number of measures to address people who might be sympathetic to that kind of radicalizing to violence message.

Mr. WILSON. Well, the grotesque nature of that statement, along with people carrying signs in English in, say, Tehran, "Death to Israel," "Death to America"—the creed of Hamas the American people need to know, and that is that "We value death more than you value life."

This is serious. I am just very concerned that the President is focused on other items, i.e., congressional campaigns, and has been missing the danger.

Based on the bulletin that was issued by DHS and FBI regarding soldiers' online media accounts, what level of danger do you feel for our military and our military families?

Mr. WARRICK. Well, as I said, there is no specific credible threat targeting specific people in a specific place.

But we do think that it is appropriate that people are prudent and that social media postings should not describe military operational activities, nor should they describe law enforcement activities or other measures.

This is something that we just caution people in our own organization and, indeed, in our military, to be prudent in what they post on social media.

But for people who take those reasonable steps, it is obviously very difficult for foreign fighters in Syria to get to the United States, and my Department is working to make it even harder for that to happen.

So what we really do is encourage people to exercise reasonable prudence. And then, obviously, there is the support that we need from communities to help be on the alert for things that they may notice at a local level far before we in the Federal Government would ever see anything.

Mr. WILSON. And with this warning by the FBI and Department of Homeland Security, are you aware of any steps that the Department of Defense has taken to alert, again, servicemembers, military families, veterans, to what threats may be?

Mr. WARRICK. The Department of Defense, we know, has guidance on that. But, obviously, I would leave it to them to describe their guidance to servicemembers about social media postings.

We just felt it was prudent for us to remind people that this is a time in which they should be prudent in measures about any activities or postings they may have.

But the Department of Defense has a number of procedures and rulings that are in place and, obviously, you can get that information from them.

Mr. WILSON. Thank you very much.

Mr. POE. Chair recognizes the gentleman from Virginia, Mr. Connally, for 5 minutes.

Mr. CONNOLLY. Thank you, Mr. Chairman.

Ambassador Bradtke, I was looking at your long and distinguished record of service to your country and the State Department. But allow me, without being disrespectful, to follow up on Mr. Sherman's question.

Do you speak Arabic?

Ambassador BRADTKE. I do not speak Arabic.

Mr. CONNOLLY. Do you have any expertise in the Arab world? Did you ever serve in the Arab world?

Ambassador BRADTKE. I don't consider that to be a primary area of expertise, but I have traveled with Secretary Christopher extensively when he was negotiating——

Mr. CONNOLLY. But you were never assigned to the region?

Ambassador BRADTKE. No. I was not assigned to the region.

Mr. CONNOLLY. So is it not true that most of the foreign fighters recruited by or attracted to ISIL in Syria come roughly from a handful of countries, mostly Arab countries? Is that not true?

Ambassador BRADTKE. Many of the foreign fighters come from North Africa, from Arab countries. That is correct.

Mr. CONNOLLY. It just—I mean, maybe you do or don't subscribe to, I think, the premise behind Mr. Sherman's question.

But as the United States moves forward, it just seems to me that the State Department needs to be promoting leadership from within that has particular focus on this region, since that is what we are dealing with.

And I mean that with no disrespect. Because sometimes somebody can function very well without any expertise in a particular subject matter because of their managerial skills, their organizational skills. Presumably, that is true about you.

But I do think that Mr. Sherman has a point, that longer term, the United States has got to get serious about this region and expertise in this region if we're going to address the challenges we face.

Let me ask a question. In looking at your seven point, you know, here is what we are doing, I didn't see a mention of strengthening our relationship with the Peshmerga and to the Kurdish community, which seems to be one of the military allies we have got in the region and has a military capacity but needs to be reinforced. Why not? Why didn't you talk about that?

Ambassador BRADTKE. If you will permit me, Mr. Connally, I do feel I want to say a word or two that your——

Mr. CONNOLLY. I have to ask you to move closer to the mic. It is very hard to hear you. Thank you.

Ambassador BRADTKE. I would like to say a word or two about your initial comments.

I was happily retired, Mr. Connally.

Mr. CONNOLLY. I saw that.

Ambassador BRADTKE. And was asked by senior officials in the State Department to come back and take this job.

I was asked to take this job not because of my expertise in Arabic or countries of the Middle East. I was asked to take this job because there was a belief that in 40 years of working for the State Department I was able to deal with a the wide variety of countries, that I could conduct dialogues with those countries on an effective basis, and that I could draw on the many experts in the State Department who are experts on those parts of the world.

This is not an effort I undertake by myself. This is an effort that I have the support of many people within the Department of State. I have found as I have traveled—I have been in Morocco, Tunisia, the UAE, Qatar, Kuwait—that I don't think the fact that I don't speak Arabic has been a hindrance.

I have had meetings with the leaders of the Islamic community in countries I have visited. The fact that I am not an expert on the Islam has not prevented, for example, when I met the leader of the Islamic community in Malaysia, I had a very good discussion with him about steps they can take to put out the word about ISIL, about ISIL's not being representative of Islamic values.

I don't feel that the discussion I had with him was in any way hindered by the fact I am not an Islamic——

Mr. CONNOLLY. Mr. Ambassador, I completely agree. That is why I really meant what I said without disrespect. I honor your career and I know you came back.

But I think Mr. Sherman has a point long-term.

This region is unraveling. It is a long-term challenge if not threat to us and to the West. It is profoundly disturbing, what is happening. We have to have expertise in the region. That is not a comment about you.

Ambassador BRADTKE. No. There is no disagreement. I believe there are some really brilliant new generation diplomats.

Mr. CONNOLLY. Good. And I——

Ambassador BRADTKE [continuing]. Who are coming up thorough the ranks, who are serving in some of our Embassies now.

Mr. CONNOLLY. I repeat, I honor you for your service. I meant no disrespect at all. I was just simply trying to reinforce this point. Now I beg you to address the Kurdish question because we are running out of time.

Ambassador BRADTKE. The reason I didn't get more deeply into that is that it is not really in my area of partner engagement on Syria foreign fighters. It is one of the lines of effort that General Allen is pursuing. I mentioned the five lines. One of those lines is support for our partners on the ground and that absolutely applies to the Kurds.

Mr. CONNOLLY. I would hope if we have another round we can get into sort of what has worked. Because I am troubled sometimes by some of the conversation we are having about, okay, when they return to a given country, what do we do? It almost sounds like deprogramming from a cult. I don't think that is going to work, given the numbers. So I would be interested in hearing from both of our witnesses about, well, are there examples of things that have worked in, A, preventing people from going, and, unfortunately, if we fail on that, helping to reintegrate them in a genuine successful way when and if they come back.

Thank you, Mr. Chairman. I know my time is up.

Mr.POE. Chair recognizes the gentleman from California, Colonel Cook.

Mr. COOK. Thank you, Mr. Chair.

Ambassador, I wanted to ask you about the role of Hamas and the Muslim Brotherhood in terms of perhaps facilitating the information on people, recruitment, in some of the smuggling activities, or if you had any insight at all from a diplomatic standpoint.

Ambassador BRADTKE. Specifically, I do not, sir, no.

Mr. COOK. No personal feelings on that terms in enabling them?

Ambassador BRADTKE. I don't have any basis on which to give you a good answer, sir.

Mr. COOK. Let me switch gears a little bit.

Chairman Poe was talking about the relationship with Turkey. And I think a number of us on this committee and the House Armed Services Committee are very, very nervous about Turkey and its reluctance to have strike aircraft be flown from Incirlik. And the other base that we have is obviously in Qatar. And it is almost like we are giving them a free pass, those two countries there, that—we are very, very nervous about there maybe have been activities in supporting ISIS and some of the other terrorist groups.

Do you have any comments at all about the Turkish situation in terms of being somewhat of a squishy ally, at least in my opinion? A member of NATO and everything else and yet I just don't trust them.

Ambassador BRADTKE. As I said earlier, I think Turkey is a very important partner of ours. It is a member of the coalition.

Mr. COOK. Have we given them a free pass on this, though?

Ambassador BRADTKE. We just had Vice President Biden in Turkey. General Allen has visited. He have had an ongoing discussion with Turkey about what we can do on the border between Turkey and Syria. Those discussions are going on. At this point, that is as much as I could say, sir.

Mr. COOK. I understand that. But every time the question comes up of smuggling and black market activities and who its buying the oil and everything, a couple of countries come up. It is like they get a free pass. And sooner or later we are going to have to—is there anybody that is reevaluating who our true allies are and who aren't?

It is almost like it is the military Stockholm Syndrome, because we have two bases in those key countries. We don't pressure them. That is basically what I am asking. Are they getting a bit of a free pass on this?

Ambassador BRADTKE. I would not say they are getting a free pass.

Mr. COOK. Okay.

Ambassador BRADTKE. We have a very strong and open dialogue with them. And that those discussions about what you were talking about, those discussions continue, and we'll have to see where that goes.

Mr. COOK. Okay. We talked about a lot of these foreign fighters coming through Turkey. How about through some of the another areas? Turkey is one area. Do they also come through—and I notice there is a large preponderance of the group from Jordan. Are these primarily from the refugee camps? Is that where they are being recruited?

Ambassador BRADTKE. The numbers of foreign fighters coming from other countries are much smaller than Turkey. Turkey is the primary transit point. Iraq, Jordan, Lebanon have lesser numbers. Obviously, in the case of Iraq and Jordan, their are efforts to curb the flow of foreign fighters. Lebanon as well, although that is somewhat more difficult situation. Goes beyond what I could talk about in this session as well.

Mr. COOK. The last question I had was in regards to the ones coming from Russia. And I suspect this relates to the Chechnya?

Is Russia facilitating their leaving the country and going to another area simply because of the problems that they are going to cause internally in Russia?

Ambassador BRADTKE. I am not aware of any evidence they are facilitating the Chechen fighters to leave Russia to get rid of them, as you just said.

Mr. COOK. Thank you very much. I yield back.

Mr. POE. Thank the gentleman.

The Chair recognizes the gentleman from New York, Mr. Higgins.

Mr. HIGGINS. Thank you, Mr. Chairman.

I think we need to forget for a moment from where these foreign fighters are coming and really ask the fundamental question which we are not asking, and that is why they are coming. ISIS' most potent recruitment tool is momentum. It is success. It is the conquest of territory covering large portions of Syria and Iraq.

ISIS' ability to sustain their momentum in their territorial conquests will determine their future recruitment from the region and from the West.

Why has ISIS been so effective in their territorial taking strategy? Because there has been no effective countervailing force to confront them. You know, the United States spent $25 billion, $26 billion building up an Iraqi Army, and during the first test, the Iraqi Army ran. Not only did we not put up a front to ISIS, they also took our weaponry that we paid for over many, many years.

So the New York Times reported this morning that there was a major deal between the Abadi government in Baghdad and the Kurdish leadership Erbil. That was a permanent, long-term deal to provide 17 percent of the national budget to the Kurdish region.

In addition, $1 billion to pay for the salaries and weapons for the Peshmerga in the Kurdistan area.

The Kurdish Army, or the Peshmerga, otherwise known as those who confront death, is estimated to be between 250,000 and 357,000 fighters. They are experienced, they are an effective army, they are pluralistic. They are proven allies of the United States in assisting us in the invasion of Iraq, they fought side by side with the American troops, they helped the United States capture Saddam Hussein.

ISIS is estimated to be between 31,000 and 41,000 fighters. This seems to be a major change in the dynamic as it relates to Iraq's ability to push back ISIS. I don't know if you caught the news of this deal this morning. But, I would like you to comment on it. Because I think unless and until you can break the momentum of ISIS, it doesn't matter where foreign fighters are coming from. The fact that they are coming is what is more important. And the success, the momentum that has been sustained by ISIS over a long period of time, is the only reason you have foreign fighters coming to Iraq and to Syria to fight, regardless of where they are coming from.

So I think this is a major breakthrough. And I would like to hear your comments on how this changes the dynamic in the region.

Ambassador BRADTKE. That question would take me well beyond my responsibilities, Mr. Higgins. I think it is better addressed to my colleagues in our Near Eastern Bureau, who are the experts on these areas. I gather there will be a subsequent hearing where they will testify. Again, I am not the expert on the Kurds, I am not the expert on the Iraq situation.

WRITTEN RESPONSE RECEIVED FROM THE HONORABLE ROBERT BRADTKE TO QUESTION ASKED DURING THE HEARING BY THE HONORABLE BRIAN HIGGINS

Regarding ISIL's momentum in Iraq, the military campaign against ISIL, which is centered on degrading ISIL from the air and defeating ISIL by working with ground forces to clear and hold territory, has halted the main ISIL offensive. Precision airstrikes by Coalition partners (the United States, Australia, Belgium, Canada, Denmark, France, The Netherlands, and the United Kingdom) have helped Iraqi central government and Kurdish forces hold or take back key terrain, and degraded ISIL's ability to mass and maneuver. The Coalition has also killed a number of ISIL's top leaders, and those who remain on the battlefield can no longer easily communicate with ISIL formations and combat units. In Mosul, ISIL's stronghold in northern Iraq, ISIL has disabled mobile phone towers to prevent Mosul residents from providing intelligence to Coalition forces and organizing attacks, but that has further degraded its own communications.

Thus far, combined operations have restored strategic sites like the Mosul Dam and Baiji Refinery to state control, held off ISIL offensives in Anbar province, strengthened the defensive corridor around Baghdad, and secured major roadways and supply routes. There is hard fighting ahead, and ISIL sometimes responds with localized offensives and atrocities, but ISIL is now being rolled back.

Ambassador BRADTKE. But I want to come back to the point you make. Yes. Clearly, the perceived success of ISIS is one reason that some people have been attracted to fight for them. But the situation in Syria itself has been a powerful magnet for——

Mr. HIGGINS. But what does ISIS depict on social media? Their success in taking over critical territory.

So if you forget about the medium, if you take away the fundamental recruitment, the emphasis, the success of ISIS, they don't really have a story to tell because a lot of this is about the narrative.

I interrupted. Continue.

Ambassador BRADTKE. I was agreeing with you that that is one very important element and why people are attracted to fight for ISIS.

But there are other factors as well. There is the situation in Syria itself. Where ISIS, al-Nusra, have made very powerful use of the idea that they are defending Sunnis inside Syria. Again, that is something we try to push back again.

Also there are other factors ranging from the idea in some cases of economics. I have been in countries where the fighters from those countries, the primary motivation is actually the idea that they can escape situations——

Mr. HIGGINS. I understand. Let me claim back my time. Respectfully, Ambassador. Let me just—because it is a very, very important point that I think is being missed. And that is combating, confronting effectively ISIS in Iraq helps us and the Free Syrian Army more effectively confront ISIS in Syria.

Ambassador BRADTKE. I don't think there is any disagreement on that point, sir.

Mr. HIGGINS. I yield back.

Mr. POE. Chair recognizes the gentleman from Florida, Mr. DeSantis, for 5 minutes.

Mr. DESANTIS. Thank you, Mr. Chairman.

Ambassador, has the State Department canceled the passports of any of U.S. citizens who have joined terrorist groups in Syria and Iraq?

Ambassador BRADTKE. To my knowledge, the State Department has not canceled any passports of——

Mr. DESANTIS. Why is that? Because we had Secretary Kerry here a couple months ago. He said he has the authority under exiting law. I think he is right about that. I know some of our allies have taken steps to cancel passports.

So what is the reasoning behind not doing that?

I ask that because the director of the FBI was on ''60 Minutes'' several weeks ago, maybe a couple months ago by now. He was asked about people that he have identified as joining ISIS or joining the al-Nusra front, and could they come back to the United States, he was asked.

He said, Well, if they have a valid passport, they are entitled to return.

A lot of my constituents were really floored by that. They would say, you go and you choose jihad, you leave America behind, you are waging jihad over there. The idea that you now have an entitlement to come back simply because you have a valid passport, and we are not going to really do much. I guess he said we would track them. But that struck me and a lot of my constituents as insufficient. So how does the State Department handle this issue?

Ambassador BRADTKE. You are correct, sir, Secretary Kerry said he does have the authority to revoke passports.

This is something we would only do in relatively rare and unique circumstances because of the importance for average Americans of the freedom to travel. We would only——

Mr. DESANTIS. And obviously an ISIS fighter would be an extreme circumstance if they are cutting off Americans' heads. So I just wanted to make sure——

Ambassador BRADTKE. May I continue, sir? We would only do it also in consultations with law enforcement authorities. We have not yet had any request from law enforcement authorities to cancel passports of ISIS or foreign fighters.

So, again, we have the authority. It is one tool. We do have other tools to use as well until this regard.

Mr. DESANTIS. No, I understand.

Ambassador BRADTKE. We would only do it in consultation with law enforcement.

Mr. DESANTIS. Mr. Warrick, maybe you can—so if a known terrorist comes back to the United States, they are being ''tracked by law enforcement,'' what does that entail? How can we be sure that they will not commit a lone-wolf attack, for example?

Mr. WARRICK. Congressman, if we have indications that someone on the No-Fly List is trying to fly back to the United States, we would deny them boarding if we have the authority to do so. Or we would recommend even to a foreign government that they or the airline deny such a person the right to get on an airplane to fly to the United States.

If someone shows up in the United States, and there is indications that that person has been a foreign fighter in Syria, it would be referred to the FBI. Then it would be a matter for law enforcement.

We would have the ability at the border to ask any questions that were necessary and appropriate. We would have the ability and the authority to inspect their luggage, inspect their personal possessions in order to determine whether they were or were not a foreign fighter who had been fighting with ISIL in Syria.

Anything like this, I can assure you, is taken extremely seriously. The notion that we are going to let somebody into the United States who is a foreign fighter just to have them monitored, sir, that is not what we are going to be working on.

Mr. DESANTIS. Well, I think his comments, maybe he didn't express himself well. But I think that was not——

What happened with Munir Mohammed Abou Saleha? He was a U.S. citizen from Florida. He went over, trained with al-Nusra Front in Syria. Then, according to the New York Times, came back to the United States for a time period and then chose to return to Syria. And he committed a suicide attack in Syria. We didn't have any intelligence on him. Is that how he was able to do that? To go over, train with al-Nusra, then come back here to the United States unimpeded?

Mr. WARRICK. The intelligence that he had been fighting with ISIL was only developed after he had departed. And certainly, obviously, you know, it is unfortunate he choose the path that he did. Had he come back into the United States, there would have been measures taken in his specific case based on the status that he had at the time we learned that he had joined ISIL.

Mr. DESANTIS. Ambassador, my final question is, a couple weeks ago it was reported in the Wall Street Journal that the President wrote a personal letter to the Ayatollah Khamenei in Iran stressing, according to the article, that there were some mutual interests between the United States and Iran with respect to fighting ISIS in Iraq.

As somebody who has served in Iraq and saw, you know, Iran and Iranian-backed terrorist groups, I mean, they killed hundreds of U.S. service members. So that was something that I flinched at.

But let me ask you: Do we consider the Iranians to be a partner of any sort in terms of fighting ISIS, even if just in the Baghdad area or throughout in the region?

Ambassador BRADTKE. I can say from my point of view I certainly do not consider Iranians to be partners in the efforts that we are undertaking.

Mr. DESANTIS. Thank you. I yield back.

Mr. POE. Chair recognizes the gentleman from Rhode Island, Mr. Cicilline, for 5 minutes.

Mr. CICILLINE. Thank you, Mr. Chairman. And thank you to the witnesses.

Ambassador, could you talk for a moment about what the impact is of foreign fighters, how they are being used? Are they engaged in actual military conflict? In suicide bombings? Or are they being used in propaganda videos? What is actually the impact of the foreign fighters and what is the magnitude of the presence of those fighters relative to the indigenous people?

Ambassador BRADTKE. Again, some of this is information that probably could be better shared in a classified setting. But let me share what I can here, my overall impressions from the work that I have been doing.

Some of this is drawn from the work that academic experts are doing, some of it is drawn from the analysis that comes from inside the U.S. Government.

The first distinction I would make is that ISIL has been more willing to take on foreign fighters. Al-Nusra, which is the al-Qaeda affiliate, has been somewhat less willing, been more selective, more careful about the foreign fighters that it has brought on. So you have first that distinction.

The foreign fighters have been used in variety of ways. Some of them have—and this is a little bit different than the foreign fighters in the case of Afghanistan and Iraq.

Very typically, in those two conflicts, the primary use for foreign fighters was as suicide bombers. I think now there a perception, although some are used as suicide bombers, that they are more valuable, that they may have skills that can be used, whether it is skills that involve social media, whether it is skills involving the repair and maintenance of equipment, whether it is medical or other skills. I think they are being put to use in those areas as well as being used as fighters themselves. And I am talking here about ISIL.

The other very disturbing thing that we have seen, and academics have—a man named Peter Neumann, who has done some very good analysis of foreign fighters, has concluded that foreign fighters are often used for some of the most distasteful, if that is the right word, things that ISIL is doing. If you noticed, for example, the beheadings, these are apparently being carried out by someone with a British accent, a U.K. person.

The analysis that Peter Neumann has of this is that because foreign fighters come to Syria, they have no real attachments, they don't speak Arabic, they are anxious to impress ISIL, they are anxious to impress the organizations, and they are willing to do things that the local recruits will not do. So we have seen that. Which I think is a very disturbing thing about the foreign fighters.

Mr. CICILLINE. Thank you. I know some prior colleague referenced U.N. Resolution 2178.

There was not only creation of a new policy, but there was a set of protocols and a framework that was created as a result of that.

Is that a successful and useful tool? What is the status of that? I mean, that imposes an obligation on countries to undertake serious efforts to prevent the ability of foreign fighters to transit. So what is the current status of that?

Ambassador BRADTKE. As I was saying earlier, 2178 is a legally binding resolution which requires countries to criminalize a variety of activities related to foreign fighters, including ones that they perhaps had not previously criminalized.

I have just come back from Indonesia, where their counterterrorism law criminalized domestic terrorists because they never had a problem with people carrying out terrorist attacks outside of Indonesia. They are now looking at how to change that law to deal with terrorists who might go to training camps outside of Indonesia.

So countries are very much looking at that resolution and trying to see where the gaps in their own legislation are.

Mr. CICILLINE. And I think it would be useful for us to have a sense of where countries are in meeting those obligations. So maybe you could follow up with the committee on that.

Ambassador BRADTKE. I have already committed to doing that, and I would be happy to do it.

Mr. CICILLINE. Thank you. Finally, I want to turn to Turkey. I know you have said that they are not complicit, though I think it is pretty clear that they have not been an enthusiastic, wonderful, reliable partner in this effort. I mean, just last week there were several foreign fighters who traveled through Turkey.

So are they, in fact, assisting us both in sharing intelligence, in counterterrorism efforts to really stop the flow of foreign fighters? You keep saying they are an important partner. I think we recognize they have value if they act the right way. But there are real questions, I think, about what they are actually doing on the ground with us.

Ambassador BRADTKE. Again, if you want a detailed analysis of exactly what our cooperation with Turkey is, you probably need to do that in a classified session. But I would say the following: We have seen increasing steps by Turkey to cut off the flow of oil, to stop the flow of foreign fighters, to get better control of their border. And the information sharing we have with the Turks has been improved.

Mr. CICILLINE. Thank you. I yield back, Mr. Chairman.

Mr. POE. Chair recognizes the gentleman from Illinois, Mr. Kinzinger, for 5 minutes.

Mr. KINZINGER. Thank you, Mr. Chairman. Thank you again for putting this together and thank you to the witnesses, thank you for being here. I appreciate it.

Let me just ask, ask you both if you can just—or whoever is better advised to answer this. I wasn't here for part of the hearing; I am sure you guys explained it. But just to explain to me briefly, very briefly, what is our policy in Syria? What are we doing there?

Ambassador BRADTKE. Again, I am not here as the administration spokesman on our——

Mr. KINZINGER. Well, you are kind of the administration guy right now in front of me. And it says you are the partner engagement on Syria foreign fighters.

Ambassador BRADTKE. That is my area of responsibility. Working with partners to deal with the foreign fighter problem. It is not to make or explain or articulate our entire Syria policy.

Mr. KINZINGER. But you have been briefed on our policy in Syria, though. Otherwise, you are in a tremendous silo right now.

Ambassador BRADTKE. Our policy—and I will give you the one-sentence answer—is to bring about a political settlement which would provide the Syrian people an opportunity to have a democratic future without Assad in power.

Mr. KINZINGER. Okay. I like the line. I mean, I do. I will point out that, in fact, during the discussion of the red line, the infamous red line 1 year ago, I was one of the vocal supporters of the need to enforce that red line. There was a lot of discussion about an offramp for Assad during that time period. You know, let's give him money and send him somewhere else. You know, let's get him out of government.

It was the failure to enforce that red line that I have not heard articulated a single serious proposal to get Assad out of office now. I agree with you, I mean, I think toppling him by force is not the best answer. The best is a peaceful transition to maintain the state. But, it is what it is right now.

So you do engage with FSA elements, am I right, in terms of being involved with foreign fighter?

Ambassador BRADTKE. I do not, no.

Mr. KINZINGER. You have no engagement with them.

Who in State does any of that? I mean, because, obviously, FSA would be a part of counter ISIS, if that is our strategy, would obviously have to be involved with the foreign fighters, and they would obviously be on the front line of why are these people are being recruited. So where does that connection happen? So if you are the foreign fighter guy, where is the——

Ambassador BRADTKE. My task, my responsibilities, the things that I have been asked to do are to pursue a diplomatic strategy with our foreign partners, our foreign countries on foreign fighters.

So I do not engage directly with the Syrian opposition. Ambassador Rubinstein is our envoy for that. Certainly others in the State Department are dealing with this issue, others in the Pentagon in terms of military and our intelligence agencies also. But I personally do not deal with that.

Mr. KINZINGER. So let me ask you this: Why is it that ISIS is attracting foreign fighters, versus foreign fighters coming to FSA, al-Nusra Front, those kinds of groups? What is it about ISIS that attracts? I mean, is it just the jihadism? What is it that you have seen?

Ambassador BRADTKE. I think it is partly the discussion I was having earlier. It is the perception that they were successful, perception that joining them is a way of trying to combat Assad. It is in some cases the way they have marketed, if that's the right word, themselves as being a place where you can come and you can be involved in this adventure. That is one of the perceptions.

It is their declaration of a caliphate, which has attracted people who misunderstand exactly what ISIL is doing and what this means.

So these are some of the factors that have caused ISIL to attract foreign fighters.

Mr. KINZINGER. I agree with you. I mean, I think that is right. I think success brings success, right? I mean, I have seen some of the ISIS propaganda. And it is powerful. It looks like, if you are a young person, if you are in your teens and you are looking for something fun to do, they make it look fun, right? Come here and do whatever you want to do, be with a bunch of guys that are out pushing this idea of jihadism and the caliphate. You can see that.

I think my concern—and you are not the guy to talk to about this, evidently—but my concern is the message that we have been sending for years about the Free Syrian Army is quite the opposite. These are the people that we actually want to be emboldened, these are the people we want to be part of a post-Assad Syria.

Instead, the message we send them, we have a lot of Members of Congress that question, that basically say they are no different than ISIS, which is actually offensive, if you have met any of these folks. Sure, anywhere on a battlefield, you are going to have allegiances switch.

But the other thing is, if you are somebody looking to overthrow Assad, what is attracting you to the FSA? There is no no-fly zone over their territories as of yet. There has been a lot of talk that the United States is helping to train and equip, but you really haven't seen it. Now the discussion is in our new-found strategy that we may train a few thousand fighters over the next year. I mean, that would not attract anybody.

So I agree with you on that. And I hope—I am not going to go past my time—but I hope that this administration really wrestles with the issue of Syria and understands you are not going to defeat

ISIS until you take care of the Syria problem. It is the incubator of the problem.

So with that, thank you for your testimony. And I yield back.

Mr. POE. Chair recognizes the gentleman from Florida, Mr. Grayson, for 5 minutes.

Mr. GRAYSON. Thank you.

Mr. Warrick, is joining ISIS a crime under U.S. law?

Mr. WARRICK. Certainly giving material support to ISIS is a violation of the Federal statutes, yes.

Mr. GRAYSON. Is that true of both U.S. citizens and non-U.S. citizens?

Mr. WARRICK. Well, I mean, the question of whether a foreign citizen violates foreign law——

Mr. GRAYSON. No. U.S. law.

Mr. WARRICK. Oh, U.S. law. We have been known to prosecute foreign nationals who are in the United States for violation of material support statutes, yes.

Mr. GRAYSON. So let's be specific about this. Let's talk, for instance, abut the 26 Irish residents or residents of Ireland who apparently have joined ISIS.

What would happen if one of them traveled to the United States?

Mr. WARRICK. Well, I am not going to get into exact hypotheticals. I do want to say, however, that where somebody has been identified as a foreign fighter fighting for ISIL in Syria, and it is possible to watch-list such a person, they are going to be in all likelihood on a no-fly list or another list of the U.S. Government that is going to attract a great deal of attention before they are allowed to get on board an airplane to the United States.

Mr. GRAYSON. Again, let's be as specific as we can. Tell us, regarding the no-fly list, what would that mean? They would never be able to many come to the United States, right?

Mr. WARRICK. Well, they wouldn't be able to fly here. The no-fly list obviously doesn't apply to other modes of transportation. However, I can assure you that there are equal or equivalent measures in place so that somebody on the no-fly list is almost certainly not going to be allowed entry into the United States if they come by cruise ship or if they fly to Canada, for example, which they may not be able to do if they are no-flied for us and they were to try, let's say, to come across the U.S. Canadian border.

Mr. GRAYSON. What are the names of those lists?

Mr. WARRICK. I'm sorry?

Mr. GRAYSON. What are the names of the lists that you are referring to, not the no-fly list, but the no-cross-the-border list.

Mr. WARRICK. Well, these are all systems managed by the Terror Screening Center, which is an arm of FBI but includes participation by DHS and others. DHS, however, has the authority to make admission decisions when someone presents him or herself at a border or at an airport. So we have the authority to refuse someone entry into the United States if they are deemed inadmissible.

There are specific grounds in the Immigration and Nationality Act that allow us to say someone who is reasonably suspected to be a terrorist or to have given material support to terrorist groups that that person can be denied entry into the United States. I can assure you, Congressman, we exercise that authority when it's appropriate for us to do so.

Mr. GRAYSON. So regardless of whether they're in a country that requires a visa or not for nationals of that country or the United States, they are simply not going to be let in. Right?

Mr. WARRICK. If they meet the standard of the Immigration and Nationality Act, we are going to comply with the law, I assure you.

Mr. GRAYSON. By not letting them in; right?

Mr. WARRICK. There are a host of footnotes and exceptions that I am not going to go into in open session. But essentially, no, we are not going to do that.

Mr. GRAYSON. Let's talk about the U.S. citizens, the ones with U.S. Passports, reputed to be 130 of them. What do we know about them? Do with we know their names, for instance.

Mr. WARRICK. You actually should ask that question to the FBI. But when they give numbers, which I would describe only as greater than 100, the numbers that you see on this chart are a private groups' estimates.

So the FBI is the better source for actual statistics. In those cases what we are talking about are identities where the name of the person is known as well as certain other information that allows us to be reasonably precise as to who it is. We at least have in mind when a decision, for instance, on someone being on a no-fly list is made.

Mr. GRAYSON. Or, for instance, when they come back. When they come back, if they are identified as a foreign fighter of ISIS, according to what you said earlier, they have committed a crime, and they can be arrested upon entry; correct?

Mr. WARRICK. That's correct.

Mr. GRAYSON. And, in fact, that has happened; correct?

Mr. WARRICK. Yes, it has.

Mr. GRAYSON. Then what happens after that? They are put in prison; right?

Mr. WARRICK. Well, first of all, they are referred to the FBI for further investigation and prosecution, that actually is outside of the DHS's purview and into the FBI's purview.

So if you want to start tracking people from that point forward, I would refer you to the FBI and then to the Department of Justice.

Mr. GRAYSON. But you are familiar with the procedures; right?

Mr. WARRICK. I am familiar with the procedures, yes.

Mr. GRAYSON. You work with the FBI to get that done; right?

Mr. WARRICK. Yes, we work very closely with the FBI and with our partners in the intelligence community. State and local law enforcement.

Mr. GRAYSON. So hearing all that, I guess we can sleep a little more soundly; right?

Mr. WARRICK. Well, sir, yes, you can. However, as we always tell everyone, prudence and vigilance is something that is the responsibility of all of us.

Mr. GRAYSON. I yield back.

Mr. POE. Chair recognizes the gentleman from Pennsylvania, Mr. Perry.

Mr. PERRY. Thank you, Mr. Chairman. Thank you, gentlemen, for your time.

Ambassador, a few months ago, taxpayers were asked to spend a couple hundred million dollars or several hundred million dollars for the training and I guess some equipping of FSA fighters.

Can you give me and us any update, we are quickly approaching the time when that proviso was to expire. What has our investment gleaned us at this point?

Ambassador BRADTKE. Again, that is an area, and there was a previous line of questioning in the same direction. I am not the person who deals with the of Free Syrian Army or the Syrian opposition, so that is really beyond my responsibilities and my mandate at the State Department.

Mr. PERRY. All right. But that is unfortunate. It is very frustrating for us, right? You come here. We have questions that we have to respond to our constituents. Either you don't have or won't give the answers. So we just walk away with nothing. So it is very frustrating.

You have no indication whatsoever, like you are not even aware where—I mean, you are aware that program is happening, and that is your complete knowledge of it? Like mine?

Ambassador BRADTKE. Again, I am not an authoritative spokesperson——

Mr. PERRY. What do you know? Do you know anything?

Ambassador BRADTKE. Congressman, I have testified here for the better part of 2 hours about what I am trying to do leading an effort to deal with foreign fighters, about our engagement with our partners, about the different approaches we are taking with those partners.

Again, I am not responsible for our overall Syria policy or our relations with the Syrian opposition. My understanding is that you have a hearing scheduled in the reasonably near future with someone who will be able to address those issues. But if there are specific questions that you want addressed, I am confident that we will find someone at the State Department who can provide you——

Mr. PERRY. Listen, I can appreciate that you have got a long record of service. And thank you very much for that.

But you must understand when you come to these things as a representative of the Department of State, you should have a modicum of information regarding many subjects, specifically the one that we are talking about. As a Member of Congress, when I go out to a town tall meeting, I can't say, well, look, I'm not involved with other appropriations; it's not my responsibility. I'll see you later. My constituents don't accept that. And with all due respect I don't feel like your answer is acceptable at this time.

But with that having been said, if you can give me the unclassified version of a long-term—unclassified—of a long-term strategy regarding a peaceful transition in Syria. Look, we have got a couple minutes here. Do the best you can. Give me the high points. I mean, Syria doesn't like us—or Turkey doesn't like Assad, so they are not helping us with ISIS. We don't like Assad or ISIS, but we picked ISIS as the more problematic one of the two at this time.

But paint some picture of where we are going. Because we just spent $500 million for Free Syrian Army fighters which we can provide no answers on, and the American people are supposed to continue to support the administration in some policy, I am asking what the heck it is.

Ambassador BRADTKE. Congressman, I was asked to come up and testify, and the subject that the testimony was to be ISIS and the threat from foreign fighters. That is what I have tried to do to the best of my ability. I was not asked to be a witness on our broader Syria policy or to be prepared to discuss the future of Syria.

I have said that the essentials of our policy are to try to have a political settlement inside Syria that enables the people of Syria to have a democratic future without Assad, that enables them to be else free from terrorist threats, from terrorist organizations as well.

I really feel that if you want to delve more deeply into our Syria policy then someone who can be an authoritative spokesman on our policy on Syria should be asked to come and testify.

Mr. PERRY. I appreciate that. Those are great platitudes that all Americans can agree with and probably all people around the world can agree with.

Let me ask you this, then: The Khorasan Group. Are you familiar? Can I ask questions about that.

Ambassador BRADTKE. I am familiar with the Khorasan Group. Some of the questions may involve classified answers, but I would be happy to try to answer your questions, sir.

Mr. PERRY. They are described as seasoned al-Qaeda operatives in Syria. Would you agree with that?

Ambassador BRADTKE. Yes, I would.

Mr. PERRY. So when al-Qaeda, seasoned al-Qaeda operatives.

So when the President told us a couple years ago that—and I don't remember the exact verbiage, but it was something similar to, al-Qaeda is decimated and on the run.

Would that comport with the success of the Khorasan Group in Syria? Or would that be counter-vening?

Ambassador BRADTKE. What I would say, sir, is that my understanding of what the President meant was al-Qaeda was an organization that had been severely damaged. That did not mean that all the individual elements of al-Qaeda had been defeated.

We see al-Qaeda in the Mahgreb, we see al-Qaeda in the Arabian Peninsula. And this group of fighters who had gone to Syria coming in some respects from Pakistan and Afghanistan, from core al-Qaeda, have tried to create space to operate in Syrian territory.

Mr. PERRY. So could I say it was a little true and maybe a little deceptive, or untrue, or whatever you want to call it, it wasn't completely factual?

Ambassador BRADTKE. I don't share your view, Congressman.

Mr. POE. The Chair recognizes the gentleman from Illinois, Mr. Schneider.

Mr. SCHNEIDER. Thank you, Mr. Chair. Again, I want to thank the witnesses for joining us today to specifically talk about the threat of foreign fighters going into Syria, vis-à-vis ISIS. Looking at the numbers that were presented to us and the sources or locations of where many of the fighters are coming from of the 16,000, roughly 5,000 are coming from North Africa, as I mentioned earlier; about another 2,500 from Europe, 40 percent of those from

France. And then from the Gulf states, you have another 4,000 roughly.

So my general question and I will ask you a couple of questions and leave you to answer—my general question is are there any common threads attracting these fighters from these different regions? Are there specific regional trends that draw those fighters and how do we with deal with that? Those are my general questions.

And Ambassador, you mentioned Peter Neumann, who released a study in the spring and specifically identified Ahmad Jibril as a cleric, a Muslim cleric who has a large following, happens to be here in the United States. Not necessarily sending people to fight, but preaching a way that inspires those folks to fight. What are we doing specifically about folks like that, not just in the United States but globally, the specific concern of people preaching from the United States? With that I will leave it to the witnesses.

Ambassador BRADTKE. Just to address briefly your question about regional trends, there are differences. I think the one common theme is the attraction of foreign fighters to the conflict in Syria. The idea that Sunni Muslims are being attacked and need to be defended. This is a fairly common theme throughout the conversations I have had with our foreign partners as to the primary reason the foreign fighters are attracted to conflict. But there are variations on this statement. In the western Balkans, for example, I have had conversations with officials there who have pointed to the fact that the foreign fighters from their countries are coming from the poorest areas, and that foreign fighters from those countries are being told if you go to Syria you will get paid, you will have a job and status.

The ideological, if you will, element is less important. I have talked to partners in Southeast Asia where, in some cases, the motivation seems more to go to get training, to get skills that can be brought back to the home country to potentially be used in terrorist activities in the home country. Again, not so much an ideological motivation. So there are regional variations to individual variations, but the most important, the most powerful motivation does seem to be the conflict in Syria, the attraction of the idea that we need to go defend our Muslim brothers, our Sunni Muslim brothers in Syria.

Mr. SCHNEIDER. If I can, the large number coming from France, almost a 1,000 fighters from France, are those residents or citizens of France who have connections to Tunisia or Morocco or Libya, or are they disconnected?

Ambassador BRADTKE. Many of them are from North Africa originally, but many of them are second or third generation. These are not necessarily first generation immigrants. And that raises another kind of regional variation.

Certainly the problem, the inability of some of our European partners to integrate their immigrant populations into their societies has left a degree of alienation that has made some of these people susceptible to the kind of propaganda that ISIL's putting out.

There is also another element here, sir, which I think can't be totally neglected. I believe it is hard to come up with specific evidence of this, but there are some foreign fighters who are simply attracted to the violence that is taking place. There was a mention of Mr. Namosh, who was alleged to have committed these killings at the Jewish Museum in Brussels. This is a man with a very deep criminal background. And again, I think there is an element of that in some of the attraction of foreign fighters, it is the attraction to violence itself.

Mr. SCHNEIDER. And as far as some of the preachers the study put out by Mr. Neumann and two others said that they specifically identified two preachers globally who were having a disproportionate influence on promoting fighters going into Syria.

Ambassador BRADTKE. I don't know whether my colleague wants to address that. The State Department does not do activities inside the United States of this nature. I am not really the right person to answer that question.

Mr. SCHNEIDER. Mr. Warrick?

Mr. WARRICK. So I am not going to obviously address the specifics of any individual case, but I do want to make the point that in all the work that we do in community outreach, working with Federal, State, and local law enforcement, we are very mindful of the distinction between those who are exercising their free speech rights and those who are, to the contrary, urging people to carry out acts of violence. The former is a protected constitutional right and the latter is a crime.

And we distinguish, in all that we do, carefully between those two characteristics. So I am not going to assess the statements of any individual religious leaders from the table here today, other than just to assure you that we are very mindful of the distinction and use that in all the work that we do.

Mr. SCHNEIDER. With that I time is expired and I yield back.

Mr. POE. The Chair recognizes the gentleman from Georgia, Mr. Collins, for 5 minutes.

Mr. COLLINS. Thank you, Mr. Chairman, I appreciate the time.

I want to follow up, Ambassador, just on a couple of quick things, because I was unable to be here for the whole time, but I have watched the hearing, and on several times, you have basically, and even with my friend from Pennsylvania, sort of punted the issue of commenting on the administration's policy on Syria. To an extent, I understand that.

I do have a question, because you are part of the policy of working with foreign fighters coming into Syria and how we deal with that, correct?

Ambassador BRADTKE. Correct.

Mr. COLLINS. Do you understand the policy of the administration? I am not asking you to comment on it, I am just asking do you understand it?

Ambassador BRADTKE. Again, I am not the authority—do I understand what the main elements are? Yes, I think I do.

Mr. COLLINS. Okay. I am not going to chase that last "I think I do." Because this is an important part to me, I am not trying to pin you down, but punting the question like the gentleman from Pennsylvania said I think is a direct issue of what we are dealing with here, because there are a lot of folks just trying to understand our policy in Syria and what we are trying to do, and for someone like my friend who has served in Iraq and served in this region during wartime this is very much of a concern. If we don't understand the policy and you are trying to carry out a bigger part of that policy, to say that you do at least attempt to understand it is encouraging.

My question is, if you understand it, what is your understanding of that policy? As short as you can be, what is your understand of the administration's policy?

Ambassador BRADTKE. The President has spoken of our policy; the Secretary of State, has spoken of our policy; Ambassador Ann Patterson who was the Assistant Secretary for the Near East and has spoken of our policy; Brett McGurk, her deputy, has spoken about the policy.

Mr. COLLINS. With all due respect, I can read theirs. I want yours, because in a job description, you are given a job, you were there to carry out your part of the policy, correct?

Okay, from your understanding of what the policy is on how we are to contain and how we are to fight and how to curb these fighters, because I have other questions on the violence aspect, which I tend to agree with you, I think they are just the soldier-of-fortune kind of attitude among some of these. They want to go, they get their experience and go.

Do you have a clear enough understanding of the policy objectives inside of Syria and then the influences to carry out your function. And if so, what do you feel like your part of that policy is?

Ambassador BRADTKE. I think I do have enough of an understanding to carry out my role, sir, because as I understand the policy, that—again, I am not the spokesperson, it is to try to bring about a political settlement in Syria that will allow the Syrian people to have a Democratic future that will be a future without Assad. That is the core, the fundamental policy. That is the basis on which I try to do what I do, which is the idea that why we are trying to deal with this foreign fighter problem, there are bigger Syria pieces that are being dealt with by the Secretary, by the President, by Ambassador Patterson, Ambassador Rubinstein, who is responsible for our Syria policy.

Mr. COLLINS. So you are actually dealing with what I think is part of the problem because there is basically a 3-prong kind of attack, however you want to look at it with the Assad regime, the fighters against Assad, and then you have the fighters against the fighters of Assad, and you have fighters coming in from all over to fight here. We did not address that. And I have read and listened to the President speak about this, we basically chose to leave the current regime sort of off the table when we are training free Syrian fighters to go after ISIS or ISIL, however you describe it, just the Islamic State. And we are saying we will deal with the Assad part of this later.

I am trying to figure out what are you doing to curb outside fighters coming in on his behalf? Is that part of your policy? And if it is, that contradicts the policy of basically leaving him for another day.

Ambassador BRADTKE. It is—certainly, most of the efforts that I have talked about here today are related to Sunni foreign fighters. They are fighters who are going to fight for ISIL or al-Nusra, the

Khorasan group, those groups. We are concerned about the other foreign fighters, if you will, that come into Syria. The Shi'a foreign fighters, the Hezbollah foreign fighters. The reality is we have fewer tools to deal with the fighters.

Mr. COLLINS. Would you say that those fighters are in it more for the fight? You know we all grew up in neighborhoods, you just had one of those guys in class, they are just going to fight. And sometimes there is a reason and sometimes there is not a reason. Would that classify more on the fighters?

Ambassador BRADTKE. I would say it again without being the expert on the subject that I feel the fighters who have gone to fight on the side of Assad are different than the fighters who are coming from other countries to fight for ISIL or al-Nusra. It is a more organized effort a supported-by-outside-countries effort.

Mr. COLLINS. Well, I appreciate your understanding because I do believe you have a difficult job and understanding the policy is important, at least your part whether you comment on the bigger part. I still think that we need to be arming those who want to fight, that is the Kurds. We need to get them involved in the fight and anybody else who wants join, you have a tough job, I commend you for doing it.

Mr. Chairman, I yield back.

Mr. POE. The Chair recognizes the patient gentlewoman from Florida, Ms. Frankel, for 5 minutes.

Ms. FRANKEL. Thank you, Mr. Chairman. I often feel like the Agatha Christie novel, And Then There Were None.

Mr. COLLINS. I have been there many times.

Ms. FRANKEL. Thank you very much gentlemen for being here. Well, this has been a very interesting discussion to listen to. And to me, it sounds like the problem is the problem, and I say that not to be facetious, but this sounds to me like one of these rock-and-a-hard place situations, not to be trite.

I think some of the frustration you have heard is there is an old saying the knee bone is attached to the thigh bone and so forth, so it is difficult for us to hear a discussion just of the foreign fighters without an overall discussion of the strategy. So I will try, out of respect, to narrow my questions to the foreign fighters, and if I ask a question that deviates, you just have to say—I will respect your answer.

So let's start with this proposition, we are to assume that these foreign fighters coming back to our country or to our allies pose an immediate present danger to our security, is that something we should assume?

Mr. WARRICK. Well, we certainly treat them as if they are a threat, if they have been a foreign fighter for ISIL, that is going to be taken with enormous seriousness. I think we do need to recognize that there is the possibility that some foreign fighters walked away from the fight because they decided that ISIL was not like it was advertised to be and its social media, which I would echo Secretary Johnson's characterization as slick, is totally at odds with the reality that people experience when they are actually fighting for ISIL. And so, undoubtedly there are people who are walking away from the fight——

Ms. FRANKEL. I have other questions, could you just answer, is it an immediate threat? I am just trying to understand the seriousness of it.

Mr. WARRICK. The answer has to be some are and we are treating everyone that way until otherwise it can be established.

Ms. FRANKEL. I want to get back to you, Ambassador. I think you said that these fighters that are coming from other countries, many of them are going to fight Assad, is that what you said?

Ambassador BRADTKE. I said I think that is one of the primary motivations.

Ms. FRANKEL. So when we go after ISIL, air strikes let's say in Iraq, when we try to denigrate ISIL, we are, in a sense, helping Assad; is that correct?

Ambassador BRADTKE. I don't think we are helping Assad. I think Assad's problems go well beyond whatever we do with ISIL. And certainly, if he is taking some consolation in the fact that we are attacking aisle I think he is making a big mistake.

Ms. FRANKEL. I am just trying to figure this out. If ISIL is coming in, the fighters are coming in to fight Assad, we are trying to denigrate ISIL, so do we encourage or incite more fighters to come in? I guess that is the question, are our actions, or our inactions, either our actions to go after ISIL inciting more fighters to come in, or our inaction to go after Assad, is that inciting more fighters to come in?

Ambassador BRADTKE. I am not sure I can give you a definitive answer here, because I can't point to specific evidence. It is hard for me to put myself in the head of a foreign fighter who sees air strikes being carried out.

Ms. FRANKEL. Well, what about in terms of the advertising that they do to bring the fighters in? Do they use our actions or inactions?

Ambassador BRADTKE. We believe they are trying to use our actions as an incentive or as a motivation for people to come and fight, but I can't point to specific evidence at this stage particularly in this setting that says whether this is, in fact, happening or not.

Ms. FRANKEL. Are most of the fighters coming in through Turkey?

Ambassador BRADTKE. Yes, Turkey is the primary——

Ms. FRANKEL. And so it seems to me another countervailing issue here is Turkey is under deluge from Syrians who are fleeing Assad. And so, their resources are hurting badly. So it seems to me that they want somebody to be fighting Assad. So do you think that that is a factor in their not keeping the borders more secure?

Ambassador BRADTKE. Turkey has made no secret that one of the primary elements of its policy is to see Assad go, but at the same time, I think Turkey also understands the threat that ISIL, in particular, poses to Turkey. We had an incident back in March where some ISIL fighters crossed over into Turkey and engaged a shootout with Turkish policemen, killing Turkish policemen.

We had ISIL kidnapping and holding hostage Turkish diplomats in Mosul, and Turkish truck drivers in Mosul. We had a case in October where Turkey broke up an ISIL group inside Turkey that had gathered weapons and explosives. So again, I think yes, Turkey wants Assad to go, that is certainly a key element of its policy, but I think at the same time, they recognize that ISIL is also a threat to Turkey itself.

Ms. FRANKEL. Thank is you, Mr. Chair. I yield back.

Mr. POE. You yield back all the time.

Thank you very much. I want to thank the gentlemen for being here for this hearing. This hearing of the joint subcommittees is concluded. Thank you.

[Whereupon, at 12:26 p.m., the subcommittees were adjourned.]

APPENDIX

Material Submitted for the Record

JOINT SUBCOMMITTEE HEARING NOTICE
COMMITTEE ON FOREIGN AFFAIRS
U.S. HOUSE OF REPRESENTATIVES
WASHINGTON, DC 20515-6128

Subcommittee on Terrorism, Nonproliferation, and Trade
Ted Poe (R-TX), Chairman

Subcommittee on the Middle East and North Africa
Ileana Ros-Lehtinen (R-FL), Chairman

TO: **MEMBERS OF THE COMMITTEE ON FOREIGN AFFAIRS**

You are respectfully requested to attend an OPEN hearing of the Committee on Foreign Affairs, to be held jointly by the Subcommittee on Terrorism, Nonproliferation, and Trade and the Subcommittee on the Middle East and North Africa in Room 2172 of the Rayburn House Office Building (and available live on the Committee website at http://www.ForeignAffairs.house.gov):

DATE: Tuesday, December 2, 2014

TIME: 10:00 a.m.

SUBJECT: ISIS and the Threat from Foreign Fighters

WITNESSES: The Honorable Robert Bradtke
Senior Advisor for Partner Engagement on Syria Foreign Fighters
U.S. Department of State

Mr. Tom Warrick
Deputy Assistant Secretary for Counterterrorism Policy
U.S. Department of Homeland Security

By Direction of the Chairman

The Committee on Foreign Affairs seeks to make its facilities accessible to persons with disabilities. If you are in need of special accommodations, please call 202/225-5021 at least four business days in advance of the event, whenever practicable. Questions with regard to special accommodations in general (including availability of Committee materials in alternative formats and assistive listening devices) may be directed to the Committee.

COMMITTEE ON FOREIGN AFFAIRS

MINUTES OF SUBCOMMITTEE ON *Terrorism Nonproliferation and Trade; Middle East and North Africa* HEARING

Day___*Tuesday*___Date___*December 2, 2014*___Room_____*2172*_____

Starting Time___*10:08 a.m.*___Ending Time___*12:26 p.m.*___

Recesses |_____| (_____to_____) (_____to_____) (_____to_____) (_____to_____) (_____to_____) (_____to_____)

Presiding Member(s)

Chairman Ted Poe

Check all of the following that apply:

Open Session ☑   Electronically Recorded (taped) ☑
Executive (closed) Session ☐   Stenographic Record ☑
Televised ☑

TITLE OF HEARING:

"ISIS and the Threat from Foreign Fighters"

SUBCOMMITTEE MEMBERS PRESENT:

Reps. Poe, Ros-Lehtinen, Chabot, Wilson, Kinzinger, Cotton, Cook, Perry, DeSantis, Collins, Meadows, Yoho, Sherman, Deutch, Connolly, Higgins, Cicilline, Grayson, Vargas, Schneider, Kennedy, Lowenthal, Frankel

---

NON-SUBCOMMITTEE MEMBERS PRESENT: *(Mark with an * if they are not members of full committee.)*

Rep. Rohrabacher

HEARING WITNESSES: Same as meeting notice attached? Yes ☑ No ☐
(If "no", please list below and include title, agency, department, or organization.)

STATEMENTS FOR THE RECORD: *(List any statements submitted for the record.)*

Statement for the Record - Rep. Connolly

TIME SCHEDULED TO RECONVENE_____
or
TIME ADJOURNED___*12:26 p.m.*___

Subcommittee Staff Director

Statement for the Record
Submitted by Mr. Connolly of Virginia

The very real potential for a radicalized U.S. citizen or someone sympathetic to the Islamic State of Iraq and the Levant (ISIL) to travel abroad to act in direct contravention of U.S. security interests and then use the protections afforded to U.S. citizens to elude authorities in returning home to carry out an attack on American soil defines the particularly insidious nature of this threat.

With estimates of the number of these so-called foreign fighters currently at 16,000 and growing from more than 80 countries, our efforts to eradicate ISIL will become a Sisyphean task if we cannot dismantle the foreign fighter network that augments enemy forces in Syria and Iraq with citizens of the United States as well as citizens of the allied countries that have joined our international coalition working to degrade and eliminate ISIL.

It is readily apparent that the U.S. response to this threat demands interagency coordination. I welcome the recent disclosure from the Department of Homeland Security (DHS) that it has formed a *Foreign Fighter Task Force*. The Federal Bureau of Investigation (FBI) has also worked diligently to identify and monitor more than 150 U.S. citizens suspected of traveling abroad to support terrorist organizations. Complicating this threat further, the same networks that are recruiting individuals to travel abroad to take up arms on behalf of ISIL are attempting to radicalize U.S. citizens here at home and motivate them to carry out an attack here on U.S. soil. The threat took another turn on Sunday, when DHS and the FBI issued a warning to current and former service members that ISIL is actively recruiting individuals to carry out attacks on members on the U.S. military.

This is a fight that will be fought on several fronts. Our law enforcement officials will be tasked with preventing U.S. citizens from travelling to Syria and Iraq to join terrorist organizations as well as identifying and intercepting Americans who have engaged in terrorist acts abroad before they have the opportunity to carry out an attack at home. In addition, the U.S. must be engaged in spurring and coordinating international efforts to prevent citizens of other countries from joining ISIL. Allies of the U.S. must demonstrate a concerted resolve to prevent the travel and recruitment of foreign fighters. Failing to do so dooms our efforts to bring stability to Syria and Iraq and potentially puts our homelands at risk.

The nature of the foreign fighter threat dictates that we pay special care to balancing security and civil liberty concerns. It is my hope that the U.S. government and its allies find innovative ways to respond to this unique threat, and leverage existing counter-terrorism protocols that have been effective in interdicting acts of terrorism. I look forward to hearing from our witnesses from the State Department and Department of Homeland Security on this and other issues as we address this emerging threat.